RHONE RIVER
CRUISE
TRAVEL GUIDE

**Exploring France's Historic Waterway from
Lyon to Avignon while Uncovering it's
Hidden Gems and Cultural Delights**

Zeke C. Xenia

TABLE OF CONTENT

CHAPTER FIVE

ACTIVITIES AND EXCURSIONS DURING YOUR RHONE RIVER CRUISE
5.1 GUIDED TOURS: CITY WALKS, HISTORIC SITES, AND HIDDEN GEMS
5.2 OUTDOOR ADVENTURES: CYCLING, HIKING, AND KAYAKING ALONG THE RHONE
5.3 CULTURAL IMMERSION: WORKSHOPS, DEMONSTRATIONS, AND LOCAL INTERACTIONS

CHAPTER SIX

MAKING THE MOST OF YOUR RHONE RIVER CRUISE
6.1 PACKING ESSENTIALS: WHAT TO BRING FOR COMFORT AND CONVENIENCE
6.2 PHOTOGRAPHY TIPS: CAPTURING THE BEAUTY OF THE RHONE VALLEY
6.3 STAYING CONNECTED: INTERNET ACCESS AND COMMUNICATION OPTIONS

CHAPTER SEVEN

BEYOND THE CRUISE: EXTENDED STAY OPTIONS
7.1 MARSEILLE: GATEWAY TO THE MEDITERRANEAN
7.1.1 Discovering Marseille's Maritime History: Vieux Port, Château d'If
7.1.2 Coastal Escapes: Cassis, Calanques National Park, and the Blue Coast
7.2 PARIS: THE CITY OF LIGHT
7.2.1 Iconic Landmarks: Eiffel Tower, Louvre Museum, Notre-Dame Cathedral
7.2.2 Cultural Immersion: Theater, Opera, and Fashion
7.2.3 Culinary Delights: Michelin-Starred Restaurants, Patisseries, and Markets

CHAPTER EIGHT

DISEMBARKATION AND FAREWELL
8.1 SAYING GOODBYE TO YOUR CRUISE EXPERIENCE

APPENDIX

USEFUL RESOURCES AND CONTACT INFORMATION

DISCLAIMER

1. Prices mentioned are close approximate and may vary depending on factors such as seasonality, tour operators, and individual preferences. It's advisable to check current prices and availability before planning your visit.

2. Many travel books tend to overwhelm you with loads of pictures, right? Well, we've intentionally chosen to mix things up a bit. You might be wondering, "What's the deal?" Here's the thing: we're all about sparking your imagination, getting your curiosity going, and getting you to dive headfirst into the enchantment of Rhone River.

By leaving out the snapshots, we're nudging you to set off on an adventure powered by the thrill of the unknown. We're not just ditching visuals for the heck of it; we're aiming to give you a richer travel experience. Through our lively storytelling and in-depth insights, we'll help you visualize the breathtaking scenery, the incredible wildlife, and the rich cultural gems of Rhone River. Trust us, it's not about taking shortcuts; it's about making your journey unforgettable.

INTRODUCTION TO THE RHONE RIVER CRUISE EXPERIENCE

A. Overview of the Rhone River: A Historical and Cultural Gem

Flowing majestically through the heart of France, the Rhone River weaves a tapestry of history and culture, enchanting travelers with its timeless beauty. Originating from the Swiss Alps, this legendary river traverses 505 miles, journeying through picturesque landscapes and centuries-old towns before meeting the Mediterranean Sea.

The Rhone has long been revered as a vital artery of trade and civilization, shaping the destinies of the regions it touches. Its banks are adorned with ancient ruins, medieval castles, and quaint villages, each bearing witness to a rich tapestry of human history.

Venturing along the Rhone, travelers are treated to a kaleidoscope of experiences, from savoring world-renowned wines in the vineyards of Burgundy to exploring the Roman ruins of Lyon. Whether you're drawn to its gastronomic delights, cultural treasures, or scenic vistas, the Rhone offers something for every discerning traveler.

B. Understanding the Appeal of Rhone River Cruises

Rhone River cruises epitomize the epitome of luxury and leisure, offering an immersive journey through the heart of France's most captivating landscapes. Unlike traditional ocean cruises, Rhone River cruises provide a more intimate and relaxed experience, with smaller vessels navigating the river's narrow channels and docking in charming ports inaccessible to larger ships.

One of the primary draws of Rhone River cruises is the opportunity to explore a diverse array of destinations without the hassle of constant packing and unpacking. From the comfort of your floating hotel, you'll seamlessly glide from one enchanting locale to the next, each day presenting new adventures and discoveries.

Moreover, Rhone River cruises offer a deeper connection to the regions they traverse, allowing travelers to immerse themselves in local culture and cuisine. Whether you're sampling fine wines in the vineyards of Provence or meandering through bustling markets in Avignon, each shore excursion promises authentic experiences that linger long after the journey ends.

C. What to Expect: A Glimpse into the Itinerary

Embarking on a Rhone River cruise is akin to embarking on a voyage of discovery, where every bend of the river reveals a new wonder waiting to be explored. While itineraries may vary depending on the cruise operator and duration of your voyage, there are several iconic destinations that are commonly featured along the Rhone.

A typical itinerary might include stops in Lyon, France's culinary capital, where you can stroll through the cobblestone streets of Vieux Lyon, UNESCO World Heritage Site, or indulge in a gastronomic feast at a traditional bouchon. Further south, you'll encounter the historic city of Avignon, home to the magnificent Palais des Papes and the iconic Pont d'Avignon.

As you continue your journey, you'll traverse the heart of Provence, where fields of lavender stretch to the horizon and charming villages beckon with their rustic charm. Highlights may include visits to the Roman ruins of Arles, immortalized by Vincent van Gogh's vibrant paintings, and the picturesque town of Viviers, with its medieval alleyways and Gothic cathedral.

Throughout your cruise, you'll have ample opportunity to partake in enriching shore excursions, from wine tastings in renowned vineyards to guided tours of ancient landmarks. Whether you're an avid history buff, a culinary connoisseur, or simply seeking relaxation amidst stunning scenery, the Rhone River offers a wealth of experiences to suit every taste and interest.

D. Budgeting for Your Rhone River Cruise: Finding the Right Fit

While Rhone River cruises are often associated with luxury and exclusivity, there are options available to suit a range of budgets and preferences. When planning your cruise, it's essential to consider factors such as the duration of the voyage, the level of accommodation, and included amenities.

Prices for Rhone River cruises can vary widely depending on these factors, with luxury cruises typically commanding higher fees than more budget-friendly options. On average, expect to pay anywhere from $2,500 to $6,000 per person for a seven-night cruise, with additional costs for optional excursions and onboard amenities.

To make the most of your budget, consider booking your cruise during the shoulder seasons of spring or fall when prices are often lower, and crowds are thinner. Additionally, look for cruise packages that include perks such as complimentary shore excursions or onboard credits, allowing you to maximize the value of your investment.

By carefully weighing your options and prioritizing experiences that align with your interests and budget, you can ensure that your Rhone River cruise is not only unforgettable but also excellent value for money.

CHAPTER ONE
PLANNING YOUR RHONE RIVER CRUISE

Embarking on a journey down the Rhone River is not just a vacation; it's an immersive experience into the heart of France's cultural and natural splendor. To ensure you make the most of this adventure, meticulous planning is key. Let's delve into the crucial aspects of planning your Rhone River cruise.

1.1 Choosing the Right Cruise Line: Options and Considerations

The first and perhaps most crucial step in planning this adventure is selecting the right cruise line. Each cruise line provides a unique experience, so understanding your options and the factors to consider will ensure your journey is everything you hope for and more.

Understanding Your Options

1. Scenic Cruises

Scenic Cruises is synonymous with luxury and all-inclusive packages. Their ships are designed to provide the utmost comfort, with spacious suites, most of which feature private balconies. Scenic goes beyond just offering a cruise; it provides an immersive experience with its Scenic Enrich program, which includes exclusive events such as private concerts in historic venues and gourmet dinners at renowned local restaurants.

Price Range: $4,000 to $10,000 per person for a 7-10 day cruise.

Key Amenities: All-inclusive pricing (including gratuities, excursions, and beverages), private butler service, multiple dining options, wellness facilities including a spa and gym, and complimentary e-bikes for onshore exploration.

2. Avalon Waterways

Avalon Waterways is known for its panoramic views and thoughtfully designed staterooms. Their "Suite Ships" feature floor-to-ceiling windows that can be opened to create an open-air balcony, allowing passengers to fully experience the stunning scenery of the Rhone River. Avalon emphasizes flexibility and personal choice, offering a range of included excursions and onboard activities.

Price Range: $2,500 to $6,000 per person for a week-long cruise.

Key Amenities: Open-air balconies, a range of included and optional excursions, onboard lectures and cultural activities, gourmet dining with locally sourced ingredients, and complimentary Wi-Fi.

3. Viking River Cruises

Viking River Cruises offers a culturally enriching experience with a strong focus on local immersion. Their itineraries include guided tours, lectures, and performances that provide deeper insights into the destinations visited. Viking's Longships are designed with a Scandinavian aesthetic, offering a serene and elegant atmosphere.

Price Range: $3,000 to $8,000 per person for a 7-10 day cruise.

Key Amenities: Included shore excursions, cultural enrichment programs, multiple dining venues, state-of-the-art staterooms with verandas, and a relaxing Aquavit Terrace for outdoor dining.

Key Considerations

1. Itinerary and Destinations

When choosing a cruise line, one of the primary considerations should be the itinerary. The Rhone River offers a variety of destinations, from the culinary capital of Lyon to the historic city of Avignon, each with its unique attractions. Evaluate the ports of call and the excursions offered to ensure they align with your interests.

Lyon: As the starting point for many Rhone River cruises, Lyon is known for its rich history, stunning architecture, and exceptional cuisine. Don't miss a visit to the UNESCO-listed Old Town and a culinary tour to sample local delicacies.

Avignon: Famous for the Palais des Papes and its vibrant arts scene, Avignon is a highlight on any Rhone itinerary. Enjoy a guided tour of the palace and explore the local markets.

Arles: Step into the world of Vincent van Gogh and Roman history. Visit the Roman amphitheater and stroll through the charming streets that inspired the famous painter.

2. Amenities and Services

Different cruise lines offer varying levels of amenities and services. Consider what is most important to you, whether it's luxurious accommodations, gourmet dining, wellness facilities, or enriching cultural activities.

Luxury and Comfort: If you prioritize luxury, look for cruise lines that offer spacious suites, private balconies, and high-end amenities like butler service and fine dining.

Culinary Experiences: For food enthusiasts, choose a cruise line known for its gourmet cuisine and culinary excursions. Scenic Cruises, for example, offers a variety of dining options and cooking classes.

Cultural Enrichment: If you're interested in learning about the local culture, opt for a cruise line like Viking that offers lectures, performances, and guided tours focused on history and culture.

3. Inclusions and Pricing

Understanding what is included in the price of your cruise is crucial for budgeting and planning. Some cruise lines offer all-inclusive packages that cover everything from meals and drinks to excursions and gratuities, while others may charge extra for certain activities and services.

All-Inclusive Packages: Scenic Cruises is an excellent choice if you prefer an all-inclusive experience. Their pricing covers almost everything, so you won't have to worry about additional costs during your trip.

Flexible Pricing: Avalon Waterways offers a more flexible approach, with many included excursions but also optional activities that you can choose to add based on your interests.

4. Ship Size and Passenger Capacity

The size of the ship and the number of passengers can significantly impact your cruising experience. Larger ships may offer more amenities and entertainment options, while smaller ships provide a more intimate and personalized experience.

Large Ships: Ideal for travelers who enjoy a wide range of onboard activities and socializing with fellow passengers.

Viking's Longships, for example, offer multiple dining venues and extensive amenities.

Small Ships: Perfect for those who prefer a quieter, more intimate atmosphere. Smaller ships like those operated by Avalon Waterways provide a more personal touch, with fewer passengers and a closer connection to the crew.

5. Reviews and Testimonials

Reading reviews and testimonials from past passengers can provide valuable insights into what you can expect from each cruise line. Look for feedback on the quality of service, the condition of the ships, the excursions offered, and the overall experience.

Online Reviews: Websites like TripAdvisor, Cruise Critic, and the cruise line's own site can be good sources of reviews. Pay attention to both positive and negative feedback to get a balanced view.

Personal Recommendations: If you know friends or family who have taken a Rhone River cruise, ask them about their experiences and any tips they might have.

Making the Final Decision

Choosing the right cruise line for your Rhone River adventure requires careful consideration of your preferences, budget, and the experiences you hope to gain. By evaluating the options and factors outlined above, you can select a cruise line that will provide a memorable and fulfilling journey through one of France's most beautiful regions.

Additional Tips for Choosing Your Cruise Line

- Consult a Travel Agent: A travel agent specializing in river cruises can provide personalized recommendations and may have access to exclusive deals and promotions.

- Join Cruise Forums: Online forums and communities, such as those on Cruise Critic, allow you to connect with other travelers who have taken similar cruises. You can gain insights and ask specific questions about different cruise lines and itineraries.
- Consider Themed Cruises: Some cruise lines offer themed cruises focused on specific interests, such as wine tasting, culinary arts, or history. These can provide a more tailored and engaging experience.
- Look for Special Promotions: Cruise lines often run special promotions and discounts, especially if you book well in advance or during certain times of the year. Sign up for newsletters from the cruise lines you're interested in to stay informed about these deals.

By taking the time to thoroughly research and consider your options, you can ensure that your Rhone River cruise is everything you've dreamed of and more.

1.2 Selecting the Ideal Itinerary: From Lyon to Avignon and Beyond

The Rhone River meanders through picturesque landscapes, charming towns, and historic cities, offering a diverse array of destinations to explore. Choosing the ideal itinerary involves balancing must-see highlights with off-the-beaten-path gems.

1. Lyon: The Gateway to the Rhone

Lyon, often referred to as the culinary capital of France, is the perfect starting point for your Rhone River adventure. As the third-largest city in France, Lyon boasts a blend of modern urbanity and historical charm, making it a must-visit destination.

Points of Interest:

- Old Lyon (Vieux Lyon): A UNESCO World Heritage site, Old Lyon is a maze of narrow cobblestone streets lined with Renaissance buildings. Don't miss the traboules, hidden passageways used by silk workers in the 19th century. Key sights include the Gothic-style St. Jean Cathedral and the Musée Miniature et Cinéma.
- Basilica of Notre-Dame de Fourvière: Perched on a hill overlooking the city, this basilica offers stunning panoramic views of Lyon. The interior is equally impressive, with intricate mosaics and stained glass windows.
- Les Halles de Lyon Paul Bocuse: Named after the famous chef Paul Bocuse, this food market is a paradise for food lovers. Sample local delicacies like praline tarts, saucisson, and a variety of cheeses.

Tips for Exploring Lyon:

- Gastronomic Experiences: Book a food tour to experience Lyon's culinary delights. These tours typically include tastings at local markets, visits to traditional bouchons (local eateries), and even cooking classes.
- Museum Visits: Allocate time to visit the Musée des Beaux-Arts, home to an extensive collection of artworks from antiquity to modern times. The museum is located at 20 Place des Terreaux, Lyon.
- Accommodation: Stay at the Cour des Loges, a luxurious hotel located in the heart of Old Lyon. It

offers a blend of historical architecture and modern amenities.

2. Vienne: Ancient Roman Heritage

A short journey from Lyon brings you to Vienne, a town steeped in Roman history. Vienne's well-preserved ancient sites make it a fascinating stop for history enthusiasts.

Points of Interest:

- Temple of Augustus and Livia: This Roman temple, dating back to the early 1st century AD, stands in the heart of Vienne and is a testament to the town's ancient past.
- Roman Theater: One of the largest Roman theaters in France, it still hosts performances and events today. The theater can accommodate up to 13,000 spectators.
- Saint Maurice Cathedral: This Gothic cathedral took over 300 years to build, resulting in a blend of architectural styles.

Tips for Exploring Vienne:

- Guided Tours: Join a guided tour to learn about Vienne's Roman history. These tours often include access to sites not open to the general public.
- Jazz Festival: If your cruise coincides with late June to early July, don't miss the Jazz à Vienne festival, one of Europe's premier jazz events.
- Dining: Enjoy a meal at La Pyramide, a Michelin-starred restaurant offering exquisite French cuisine.

3. Tournon-sur-Rhône and Tain-l'Hermitage: Wine Country Delights

Next, your cruise will take you to the twin towns of Tournon-sur-Rhône and Tain-l'Hermitage, located on opposite banks of the river. This region is renowned for its exceptional wines.

Points of Interest:

- Cité du Chocolat Valrhona: Located in Tain-l'Hermitage, this chocolate museum is a must-visit for chocolate lovers. Learn about the chocolate-making process and enjoy tastings.
- Wine Tasting: Visit the prestigious Hermitage vineyards, famous for producing some of the best Syrah wines. Many local wineries offer tours and tastings.
- Château de Tournon: This medieval castle in Tournon-sur-Rhône offers stunning views of the river and surrounding vineyards. The castle also houses a museum.

Tips for Exploring Tournon-sur-Rhône and Tain-l'Hermitage:

- Wine Tours: Book a guided wine tour that includes visits to multiple vineyards and a chance to meet the winemakers. These tours often include lunch and tastings of several vintages.
- Cycling: Rent a bike and explore the scenic cycling routes through the vineyards. The ViaRhôna cycle path runs through this region, offering breathtaking views.
- Accommodation: Stay at the Hôtel Pavillon de l'Hermitage in Tain-l'Hermitage, a charming hotel

known for its excellent service and proximity to the vineyards.

4. Avignon: City of Popes and Palaces

Avignon, known as the City of Popes, is one of the most iconic stops on the Rhone River. Its historical significance and architectural beauty make it a highlight of any Rhone River cruise.

Points of Interest:

- Palais des Papes: This massive Gothic palace was the residence of several popes during the 14th century. It's one of the largest and most important medieval Gothic buildings in Europe.
- Pont d'Avignon: Also known as the Pont Saint-Bénézet, this historic bridge is famous for the French song "Sur le Pont d'Avignon." Only a few arches remain, but it's a fascinating site to visit.
- Avignon Cathedral: Located next to the Palais des Papes, this Romanesque cathedral is known for its beautiful interior and the golden statue of the Virgin Mary on its tower.

Tips for Exploring Avignon:

- Cultural Events: Plan your visit during the Avignon Festival in July, one of the most important contemporary performing arts festivals in the world.
- Dining: Dine at La Fourchette, a renowned restaurant offering Provencal cuisine. Make sure to book a table in advance.
- Accommodation: Stay at the Hotel d'Europe, a luxurious hotel with a rich history dating back to the 16th century. It's located at 12 Place Crillon, Avignon.

5. Arles: Inspiring Van Gogh's Masterpieces

Arles, a city that inspired many of Vincent van Gogh's works, is another must-visit on your Rhone River itinerary. Its Roman monuments and artistic heritage are captivating.

Points of Interest:

- Arles Amphitheater: This well-preserved Roman amphitheater is still used for events today, including bullfighting and concerts.
- Espace Van Gogh: Visit the former hospital where Van Gogh was treated, now a cultural center dedicated to his life and works.
- Alyscamps: This ancient Roman necropolis is a hauntingly beautiful site that inspired several of Van Gogh's paintings.

Tips for Exploring Arles:

- Art Tours: Follow in the footsteps of Van Gogh with a guided tour of the sites that inspired his paintings. The Fondation Vincent van Gogh Arles also hosts contemporary art exhibitions.
- Photography: Arles is a UNESCO World Heritage site known for its photogenic Roman and Romanesque monuments. Bring your camera to capture the stunning architecture.
- Dining: Enjoy a meal at L'Atelier de Jean-Luc Rabanel, a Michelin-starred restaurant offering creative and refined cuisine. Reservation is recommended.

6. Viviers: Medieval Tranquility

Viviers is a small but charming medieval town that offers a tranquil respite on your Rhone River cruise. Its narrow streets and historical buildings are a delight to explore.

Points of Interest:

- Saint Vincent Cathedral: The smallest cathedral in France, this Romanesque-Gothic structure is a hidden gem with beautiful stained glass windows.
- Old Town: Wander through the well-preserved old town with its narrow streets, ancient houses, and charming squares.
- Bishop's Palace: This impressive building offers insight into the town's ecclesiastical history and provides panoramic views of the surrounding countryside.

Tips for Exploring Viviers:

- Walking Tours: Join a guided walking tour to learn about Viviers' rich history and architecture. The local tourist office offers several options.
- Relaxation: Take time to simply stroll through the town and enjoy its peaceful atmosphere. Stop by a local café for a coffee and soak in the medieval charm.
- Accommodation: Stay at the Hôtel Le Prieuré, a historic hotel offering comfortable rooms and a lovely garden.

7. Beaune: Wine Capital of Burgundy

Although not directly on the Rhone River, Beaune is a short excursion away and is well worth a visit. Known as the wine capital of Burgundy, Beaune is famed for its historic sites and exceptional wines.

Points of Interest:

- Hôtel-Dieu: This medieval hospital, with its distinctive glazed tile roof, is now a museum showcasing the history of Beaune and Burgundy wine.
- Wine Cellars: Visit the extensive wine cellars of renowned producers such as Maison Joseph Drouhin and Bouchard Père & Fils. These tours often include tastings of prestigious vintages.
- Basilica of Notre-Dame: This Romanesque church is known for its beautiful architecture and stunning tapestries.

Tips for Exploring Beaune:

- Wine Tours: Book a wine tour that includes visits to several vineyards and cellars. Many tours also offer the chance to meet the winemakers and learn about the wine-making process.
- Market Visit: Explore the bustling market in Beaune's town center, where you can sample local cheeses, cured meats, and freshly baked pastries. The market is held on Saturdays.
- Accommodation: Stay at the Hôtel Le Cep, a luxury hotel located in the heart of Beaune's historic district. It offers elegant rooms, a gourmet restaurant, and a spa.

1.3 When to Go: Weather, Seasons, and Special Events

Understanding the climate patterns, peak seasons, and unique local festivities can help you choose the perfect time for your journey. Here's a detailed guide to navigating the seasons along the Rhone River.

1. Spring (March to May)

Spring is an enchanting time to embark on a Rhone River cruise, as the region awakens from its winter slumber. Mild temperatures and blossoming landscapes make it an ideal season for outdoor activities and sightseeing.

Weather and Scenery:

Temperature: Average temperatures range from 10°C (50°F) in early March to 20°C (68°F) in May, providing comfortable weather for exploring both on and off the ship.

Scenery: Expect to see vibrant blooms, lush greenery, and blossoming vineyards. The countryside is particularly picturesque, with fields of flowers and budding grapevines.

Special Events and Activities:

Festival of Violets in Tourrettes-sur-Loup: Held in March, this colorful festival celebrates the arrival of spring with vibrant floral displays, parades, and markets dedicated to violets. It's a delightful opportunity to immerse yourself in local culture and enjoy the fragrant beauty of the season.

Wine Tasting and Vineyard Tours: Spring is an excellent time for wine enthusiasts to visit vineyards and participate in tasting sessions. The Côtes du Rhône region, famous for its exceptional wines, offers numerous tours where you can learn about wine production and sample the latest vintages.

Tips for Spring Travel:

- Pack layers to accommodate fluctuating temperatures. Include a light jacket or sweater for cooler mornings and evenings.
- Be prepared for occasional rain showers by packing a compact umbrella or raincoat.
- Take advantage of fewer crowds compared to the peak summer season, allowing for a more relaxed and intimate experience at popular attractions.

2. Summer (June to August)

Summer is the peak tourist season along the Rhone River, characterized by warm weather, long daylight hours, and a bustling atmosphere. This is the perfect time for travelers who enjoy vibrant festivals and outdoor activities.

Weather and Scenery:

Temperature: Average temperatures range from 20°C (68°F) to 30°C (86°F), with July and August being the hottest months. Expect plenty of sunshine and clear skies.

Scenery: The landscape is at its most lush and verdant, with flourishing vineyards and fields of sunflowers. The riverbanks are alive with activity, offering stunning views from the cruise ship.

Special Events and Activities:

Avignon Festival: Held in July, the Avignon Festival is one of the most important cultural events in France, featuring theater performances, dance shows, and concerts. The entire city transforms into an open-air stage, attracting artists and audiences from around the world.

Tour de France: The iconic cycling race often passes through the Rhone Valley in July. Witnessing the race in person is a thrilling experience, and many towns along the river host special events and celebrations in conjunction with the tour.

Arles Feria du Riz: In early September, the town of Arles celebrates its rice harvest with a lively feria, including bullfights, parades, and traditional music and dance. This event offers a unique glimpse into the region's agricultural heritage and festive spirit.

Tips for Summer Travel:

- Book your cruise and excursions well in advance to secure your preferred dates and avoid disappointment.
- Pack lightweight, breathable clothing to stay comfortable in the warm weather. Don't forget sunscreen, sunglasses, and a hat for sun protection.
- Prepare for larger crowds at popular sites and attractions, especially in major cities like Lyon and Avignon. Consider exploring lesser-known towns and villages for a more tranquil experience.

3. Fall (September to November)

Fall is a fantastic time to cruise the Rhone River, with cooler temperatures, stunning autumn foliage, and the grape harvest season. It's a perfect blend of pleasant weather and cultural experiences.

Weather and Scenery:

Temperature: Average temperatures range from 15°C (59°F) in September to 10°C (50°F) in November. The weather remains generally mild, though evenings can be chilly.

Scenery: The fall foliage is breathtaking, with shades of red, orange, and yellow painting the landscape. Vineyards are busy with the grape harvest, adding a touch of authenticity to your wine-tasting excursions.

Special Events and Activities:

Vendanges (Grape Harvest): September marks the start of the grape harvest season in the Rhone Valley. Many vineyards open their doors to visitors, offering harvest tours and the chance to participate in grape picking. It's a hands-on way to learn about winemaking and enjoy freshly harvested grapes.

Beaujolais Nouveau Festival: Celebrated on the third Thursday of November, this festival marks the release of the new Beaujolais wine. Towns and villages across the region host parties and tastings, providing a festive atmosphere and a taste of the year's first wine.

Fête des Lumières in Lyon: Held in early December, this spectacular light festival illuminates the city with stunning displays and installations. Buildings, streets, and parks are transformed into works of art, creating a magical experience for visitors.

Tips for Fall Travel:

- Dress in layers to adapt to changing temperatures. Include a warm jacket or coat for cooler evenings.
- Take advantage of the quieter tourist season to enjoy a more relaxed pace and reduced prices on cruises and accommodations.

- Explore local markets and food festivals to sample seasonal produce and regional specialties.

4. Winter (December to February)

Winter cruises along the Rhone River offer a unique and tranquil experience, with fewer tourists and a serene atmosphere. While some attractions may have limited hours, there are still plenty of festive activities to enjoy.

Weather and Scenery:

Temperature: Average temperatures range from 5°C (41°F) to 10°C (50°F). While the weather is cooler, it rarely dips below freezing, making it a pleasant time for sightseeing.

Scenery: The winter landscape is peaceful and often adorned with festive decorations. Snow is rare but can add a magical touch to the scenery.

Special Events and Activities:

Christmas Markets: Towns along the Rhone River, such as Lyon, Avignon, and Arles, host charming Christmas markets in December. These markets feature artisanal crafts, festive foods, and holiday decorations, creating a delightful holiday atmosphere.

New Year's Eve Celebrations: Ring in the New Year with fireworks, live music, and celebrations in cities like Lyon and Avignon. Cruise ships often host special gala dinners and parties for guests to enjoy.

Truffle Hunting: Winter is truffle season in the Rhone Valley. Join a guided truffle hunting excursion to learn about these prized fungi and enjoy tastings of truffle-infused dishes.

Tips for Winter Travel:

- Pack warm clothing, including a hat, gloves, and scarf, to stay comfortable during outdoor activities.
- Check the operating hours of attractions and restaurants, as some may have reduced hours or seasonal closures.
- Enjoy the festive atmosphere and unique cultural experiences that winter brings, from Christmas markets to cozy evenings onboard.

Practical Information

1. Lyon: The starting point for many Rhone River cruises. Known for its rich history, gastronomy, and vibrant cultural scene.

- Address: Lyon, France
- Notable Attractions: Basilica of Notre-Dame de Fourvière, Old Lyon, and Les Halles de Lyon Paul Bocuse.

2. Avignon: Famous for its medieval architecture and the Palais des Papes.

- Address: Avignon, France
- Notable Attractions: Palais des Papes, Pont d'Avignon, and the Avignon Festival.

3. Arles: A city with a rich Roman heritage and connections to Vincent van Gogh.

- Address: Arles, France
- Notable Attractions: Roman Amphitheater, Van Gogh Trail, and Les Alyscamps.

4. Vienne: Known for its Roman ruins and vibrant cultural scene.

- Address: Vienne, France
- Notable Attractions: Temple of Augustus and Livia, Ancient Theater, and the Jazz à Vienne Festival.

5. Beaune: The wine capital of Burgundy, renowned for its historic buildings and wine cellars.

- Address: Beaune, France
- Notable Attractions: Hôtel-Dieu Museum, Wine Cellars, and the Hospices de Beaune Wine Auction.

1.4 Booking Your Cruise: Tips for Securing the Best Deals

Booking your Rhone River cruise requires careful consideration of pricing, promotions, and additional perks offered by cruise lines and travel agents. By being proactive and strategic, you can maximize savings without compromising on quality.

1. Book Early

One of the most effective ways to secure a good deal on your Rhone River cruise is to book early. Cruise lines often offer early booking incentives to encourage travelers to reserve their spots well in advance. These incentives can include discounted fares, free cabin upgrades, and onboard credits.

For example, Avalon Waterways offers early bird discounts that can save you up to $1,000 per person if you book at least six months in advance. Viking River Cruises might offer reduced rates or free airfare for early bookings. By planning ahead, you can lock in these deals and enjoy significant savings.

2. Stay Flexible with Dates and Itineraries

Flexibility is a valuable asset when booking a cruise. Prices for Rhone River cruises can vary greatly depending on the time of year, day of the week, and specific itinerary. If you can be flexible with your travel dates, you'll have a better chance of finding lower rates.

For instance, traveling during the shoulder seasons—spring (March to May) and fall (September to November)—can often yield lower prices compared to the peak summer months. During these periods, you'll not only save money but also enjoy fewer crowds and milder weather. Additionally, consider mid-week departures, as these are often less expensive than weekend sailings.

3. Monitor Promotions and Flash Sales

Cruise lines and travel agencies frequently run promotions and flash sales, offering substantial discounts for a limited time. These sales can include last-minute deals, seasonal discounts, or exclusive offers for certain destinations. To take advantage of these opportunities, sign up for newsletters from cruise lines and travel agencies, follow their social media channels, and regularly check their websites.

For example, Uniworld Boutique River Cruises occasionally offers flash sales where you can save up to 50% on select sailings. Viking River Cruises might have limited-time offers that include free or discounted airfare. By staying informed and ready to act quickly, you can secure fantastic deals.

4. Consider Package Deals

Many cruise lines offer bundled packages that include additional services such as airfare, pre- or post-cruise hotel stays, and guided tours. These packages can provide excellent value and simplify your travel planning. When comparing prices, consider the total cost of individual components versus the package price to ensure you're getting a good deal.

For instance, Scenic Cruises offers all-inclusive packages that cover not only the cruise fare but also flights, transfers, excursions, meals, and beverages. While the upfront cost may seem higher, the comprehensive nature of these packages often results in overall savings.

5. Use a Travel Agent

Travel agents can be an invaluable resource when booking a Rhone River cruise. They have access to exclusive deals, promotions, and group rates that may not be available to the general public. Additionally, travel agents can provide expert advice, help you navigate the various options, and assist with any issues that may arise before or during your trip.

For example, an experienced travel agent might be able to secure a special group rate for a family reunion or a themed cruise. They can also alert you to upcoming promotions and help you take advantage of loyalty programs if you've cruised with a particular line before.

6. Join Loyalty Programs

If you're a frequent cruiser, joining a cruise line's loyalty program can offer significant benefits. These programs often provide exclusive discounts, priority bookings, cabin upgrades, and onboard credits. Even if you're new to cruising, signing up for a loyalty program can still yield advantages for future trips.

For example, Viking River Cruises' Explorer Society offers members discounts on future sailings, invitations to special events, and early access to new itineraries. Scenic Cruises' loyalty program, Scenic Club, provides benefits such as priority booking, exclusive offers, and points that can be redeemed for rewards.

7. Book Last-Minute Deals

While booking early has its advantages, being open to last-minute deals can also lead to substantial savings. Cruise lines often lower prices as the departure date approaches to fill any remaining cabins. If you have flexible travel plans and can be ready to go on short notice, this strategy can be quite rewarding.

Websites like Last Minute Cruises or the "Deals" section on individual cruise line websites can help you find these opportunities. Keep in mind that last-minute deals may have limited cabin options and fewer amenities, so weigh the pros and cons before booking.

8. Compare Prices and Inclusions

Not all cruise deals are created equal, so it's important to compare prices and what's included in the fare. Look beyond the base price and consider factors such as cabin size, onboard amenities, included excursions, dining options, and gratuities.

For instance, a lower-priced cruise may not include excursions or beverages, which can add up to significant additional costs. On the other hand, a slightly higher-priced cruise that includes all these elements might offer better overall value. Make a list of your must-have amenities and compare the total cost of each option.

9. Travel Off-Peak

Traveling during off-peak times can lead to substantial savings. As mentioned earlier, shoulder seasons like spring and fall are great times to book a Rhone River cruise for lower prices and fewer crowds. Additionally, consider booking during non-holiday periods and avoiding major school vacation times when prices tend to be higher.

For example, cruising in late September can be a wonderful experience with pleasant weather and the beginning of the grape harvest season in the Rhone Valley. Not only will you find better deals, but you'll also enjoy a more relaxed and authentic travel experience.

10. Take Advantage of Group Rates

If you're traveling with a group of friends or family, inquire about group rates and benefits. Many cruise lines offer discounts for groups, as well as additional perks such as private tours, complimentary amenities, or even free cruises for the group organizer.

For instance, booking a group of 10 or more with AmaWaterways can unlock special group pricing and amenities, such as a private cocktail party or a dedicated group coordinator on board. Group travel can be a cost-effective and enjoyable way to experience the Rhone River together.

11. Utilize Credit Card Rewards and Points

If you have a travel rewards credit card, consider using your points or miles to offset the cost of your cruise. Many credit card companies offer travel booking services where you can redeem points for cruises, flights, and hotel stays. Additionally, some credit cards offer special benefits for travel purchases, such as travel insurance, purchase protection, and no foreign transaction fees.

For example, the Chase Sapphire Preferred Card allows you to redeem points through the Chase Ultimate Rewards portal for travel bookings, including cruises. You might also earn bonus points on travel-related purchases, helping you accumulate more points for future trips.

12. Read the Fine Print

Before finalizing your booking, make sure to read the fine print and understand the terms and conditions. Pay attention to cancellation policies, change fees, and any additional costs that may not be immediately apparent. Knowing the details can prevent unexpected expenses and ensure a smooth booking process.

For example, some cruise lines may charge hefty fees for cancellations or changes made close to the departure date. Others might have specific terms regarding included amenities or excursion availability. Being informed about these details will help you make a more confident and informed booking decision.

1.5 Preparing for Your Trip: Essential Packing List and Travel Documents

As you embark on your Rhone River cruise adventure, proper preparation is essential to ensure a smooth and enjoyable journey. From packing essentials to necessary travel documents, here's what you need to know before setting sail.

1. Book Early

One of the most effective ways to secure a great deal on a Rhone River cruise is to book early. Cruise lines often offer early booking incentives, such as discounted fares, cabin upgrades, or onboard credits, to encourage travelers to reserve their spots well in advance.

- Why It Works: Cruise lines benefit from having a full roster of passengers early on, allowing them to plan and allocate resources efficiently. To incentivize early bookings, they offer special deals that can save you a significant amount of money.
- Example: Avalon Waterways, for instance, frequently offers early bird discounts of up to 10-15% off the regular fare if you book six to twelve months in advance.
- Tip: Set a reminder to start researching cruise options as soon as they are released, usually 18-24 months before departure. This gives you the best chance to snag early booking deals.

2. Stay Flexible

Flexibility with your travel dates can also lead to substantial savings. Cruise prices can vary significantly depending on the season, day of the week, and availability. By being open to different departure dates, you increase your chances of finding a lower fare.

- Why It Works: Just like airlines, cruise lines adjust their pricing based on demand. Off-peak times, such as late fall or early spring, often see fewer travelers, leading to lower prices.
- Example: Viking River Cruises may offer lower rates for departures in April or October compared to peak summer months. A cruise that costs $4,500 in July might drop to $3,200 in October.
- Tip: Use flexible date search tools on booking websites to compare prices across a range of dates.

Additionally, consider mid-week departures, which can be less expensive than weekend starts.

3. Look for Package Deals

Many cruise lines and travel agencies offer bundled packages that include airfare, pre- or post-cruise hotel stays, and guided tours at a discounted rate. These packages can provide excellent value and simplify the planning process.

- Why It Works: Bundling services allows companies to offer lower prices than booking each component separately. It also ensures a seamless travel experience with coordinated logistics.
- Example: Companies like Scenic Cruises offer packages that include round-trip airfare from major cities, hotel stays in Lyon before embarking, and guided city tours. Such a package might save you up to 20% compared to booking each component individually.
- Tip: When considering a package, calculate the total cost of booking each element separately to ensure the bundle offers genuine savings. Also, check what's included in the package to avoid surprises.

4. Monitor Promotions

Keep an eye out for flash sales, limited-time offers, and exclusive discounts from travel agents and online booking platforms. Signing up for newsletters or following cruise lines on social media can keep you informed about these deals.

- Why It Works: Cruise lines and travel agencies regularly launch promotions to fill remaining cabins or boost sales during slow booking periods. These promotions can include reduced fares, free excursions, or onboard credits.

- Example: Emerald Waterways might offer a flash sale with a 25% discount on select Rhone River cruises booked within a specific 48-hour window.
- Tip: Sign up for multiple cruise line newsletters and follow their social media accounts. Use price alert tools on booking websites to receive notifications when prices drop.

5. Consider Group Bookings

Traveling with a group can unlock additional discounts and perks. Whether it's a family reunion, a group of friends, or an organized tour, group bookings often come with benefits such as complimentary amenities or private excursions.

- Why It Works: Cruise lines offer group discounts to encourage larger bookings. They benefit from the guaranteed revenue and reduced marketing costs associated with securing multiple cabins at once.
- Example: Booking five or more cabins with Uniworld River Cruises might entitle your group to a 10% discount, free onboard credits, and a complimentary group photo package.
- Tip: When planning a group trip, appoint a group coordinator to handle communications with the cruise line. This person can negotiate directly with the cruise operator to secure the best deals and additional perks.

6. Leverage Travel Agents

Travel agents can be invaluable allies in securing the best cruise deals. Their industry connections and expertise can help you find exclusive discounts and promotions that might not be available to the general public.

- Why It Works: Travel agents often have access to special rates and packages through their relationships with cruise lines. They can also provide personalized advice and assistance, making the booking process smoother.
- Example: A travel agent might have access to a limited-time promotion from Tauck River Cruises that includes a free two-night stay in Lyon before the cruise, saving you hundreds of dollars.
- Tip: Choose a travel agent who specializes in river cruises and has a proven track record of securing great deals for their clients. Don't hesitate to ask about any exclusive offers they can provide.

7. Use Credit Card Points and Rewards

If you have accumulated points or rewards through your credit card, you might be able to redeem them for significant savings on your Rhone River cruise. Many credit card companies offer travel rewards programs that include cruises.

- Why It Works: Redeeming points for travel expenses can significantly reduce the out-of-pocket cost of your cruise. Some credit cards also offer additional travel perks such as travel insurance or priority boarding.
- Example: If you have a Chase Sapphire Preferred card, you can use your points to book a cruise through the Chase Ultimate Rewards portal at a favorable rate. For instance, 60,000 points could cover $750 worth of cruise fare.
- Tip: Review the terms and conditions of your credit card's rewards program to understand how to maximize your points. Ensure there are no blackout dates or restrictions that could affect your booking.

8. Take Advantage of Last-Minute Deals

If you have the flexibility to travel on short notice, last-minute deals can offer substantial savings. Cruise lines often reduce prices for unsold cabins as the departure date approaches.

- Why It Works: Rather than sailing with empty cabins, cruise lines prefer to fill them at a lower price. This can lead to significant discounts for last-minute bookings.
- Example: AmaWaterways might offer last-minute deals with savings of up to 50% for cruises departing within the next 30-60 days.
- Tip: Check cruise line websites regularly for last-minute offers, and be ready to book quickly when you find a good deal. Keep your travel documents and essentials ready for a prompt departure.

9. Join Loyalty Programs

If you've cruised with a particular line before, joining their loyalty program can provide you with additional discounts and perks. Many cruise lines reward repeat customers with exclusive offers and benefits.

- Why It Works: Loyalty programs incentivize repeat business by offering members exclusive discounts, priority booking, and other benefits that enhance the cruise experience.
- Example: Viking River Cruises' Explorer Society offers members benefits such as discounts on future cruises, onboard amenities, and special events.

- Tip: Sign up for the loyalty program of your preferred cruise line as soon as possible to start accruing points and enjoying member benefits on your first cruise.

10. Comparison Shopping

Don't settle for the first deal you find. Comparison shopping across different platforms can help you find the best price and the most comprehensive package for your needs.

- Why It Works: Different booking platforms and travel agencies may offer varying prices and promotions. By comparing options, you can identify the best deal available.
- Example: Compare prices on major travel booking websites like Expedia, Travelocity, and directly on the cruise line's official site. A cruise that costs $3,800 on one site might be available for $3,500 on another.
- Tip: Use comparison websites that aggregate prices from multiple sources, and consider booking directly with the cruise line if they offer a price match guarantee.

11. Off-Peak Travel

Traveling during off-peak times can also lead to significant savings. The Rhone River cruise season typically runs from April to October, with peak travel occurring in the summer months.

- Why It Works: Off-peak travel periods, such as early spring or late fall, often see reduced fares due to lower demand. Additionally, the destinations may be less crowded, enhancing your overall experience.

- Example: A cruise in May with CroisiEurope might cost $3,000, while the same itinerary in July could rise to $4,200.
- Tip: Research the climate and seasonal events of your intended travel dates to ensure you're comfortable with the weather and any potential limitations on activities.

12. Utilize Online Forums and Communities

Engaging with online travel forums and communities can provide insider tips and recommendations for finding the best cruise deals. Fellow travelers often share their experiences and alert others to current promotions.

- Why It Works: Forums and travel communities are excellent resources for real-time information and personal experiences. They can offer firsthand insights that are not available through official channels.
- Example: Websites like Cruise Critic and TripAdvisor have active forums where members discuss deals, share reviews, and provide advice on securing the best prices.
- Tip: Participate in discussions and ask questions about current promotions or strategies for finding deals. Experienced travelers are usually happy to share their knowledge.

Booking your Rhone River cruise with a focus on securing the best deals can significantly enhance your overall experience by allowing you to allocate more resources to onshore activities and indulgences. By employing these strategies,you can unlock savings, added perks, and a sense of satisfaction knowing you got the most value for your money. Whether you're a seasoned cruiser or embarking on your first river adventure, these tips will help you navigate the booking process with confidence and ease.

Remember to start your planning early to take advantage of early booking incentives and keep an eye out for promotions and flash sales. Stay flexible with your travel dates and consider alternative departure times to access lower pricing options. Don't hesitate to explore package deals that bundle airfare, hotel stays, and excursions for added convenience and savings.

CHAPTER TWO
EMBARKING ON YOUR RHONE RIVER ADVENTURE

2.1 Boarding Your Cruise Ship: First Impressions and Welcome Aboard

Arrival and Initial Impressions

As your taxi or shuttle bus pulls up to the dock, the sight of your Rhone River cruise ship is sure to evoke a sense of excitement and anticipation. The ships used for river cruising are typically sleek, elegant vessels that blend modern design with timeless charm. Unlike the colossal ocean liners, these ships are more intimate, allowing for a more personal and immersive experience.

The embarkation process usually starts in the early afternoon, around 1:00 PM to 3:00 PM. However, it's wise to check your specific cruise line's guidelines and aim to arrive early to avoid any rush. When you arrive at the port, porters will greet you to assist with your luggage, ensuring it is swiftly transported to your cabin.

The Check-In Process

Upon arrival at the embarkation terminal, you will proceed to the check-in area. Here, you will need to present your travel documents, including your passport, cruise ticket, and any required health forms. Some cruise lines might also require proof of vaccination or a negative COVID-19 test, depending on the current travel guidelines. It's always best to check these requirements well in advance.

The check-in process is designed to be smooth and efficient. You'll be assigned a boarding group and provided with a keycard, which serves multiple purposes: it's your cabin key, onboard credit card, and identification card. Hold onto this card carefully, as it's essential throughout your cruise.

Welcome Aboard: First Impressions

As you step onboard, you're immediately struck by the welcoming atmosphere and elegant interiors. The ship's lobby, often adorned with stylish decor and comfortable seating areas, sets the tone for the luxury and comfort you'll experience throughout your journey. Friendly crew members, dressed in crisp uniforms, greet you warmly, offering a welcome drink – usually a glass of sparkling wine or a refreshing cocktail.

One of the first things you'll notice is the attention to detail in the ship's design. From the plush carpets to the polished wood finishes and tasteful artwork, everything exudes a sense of sophistication. Large windows line the common areas, providing stunning views of the river and the landscapes beyond, ensuring you're never far from the beauty of the Rhone.

Orientation and Ship Tour

Shortly after boarding, many cruise lines offer a guided tour of the ship. This orientation session is invaluable, especially if it's your first river cruise. The tour typically covers key areas of the ship, including:

- The Main Lounge: The social hub of the ship, where you'll enjoy evening entertainment, lectures, and socializing with fellow passengers. The lounge often features a bar, comfortable seating, and panoramic windows.

- The Dining Room: Where you'll savor delicious meals prepared by skilled chefs. Dining rooms on river cruise ships are designed for an intimate dining experience with elegant table settings and attentive service.
- Sun Deck: The top deck of the ship, equipped with lounge chairs, shaded areas, and sometimes even a small pool or hot tub. The sun deck is perfect for relaxing, sunbathing, and taking in the scenic views.
- Fitness Center and Spa: For those who like to stay active, the fitness center offers a range of equipment, while the spa provides a sanctuary for relaxation with various treatments available.
- Library and Reading Room: A quiet space filled with books, magazines, and comfortable seating, ideal for unwinding with a good book.

During the tour, the crew will also point out important safety features, such as emergency exits, muster stations, and life jackets. Familiarizing yourself with these locations is crucial for your safety.

Your Cabin: A Cozy Retreat

After the tour, it's time to find your cabin and settle in. The cruise line's staff will direct you to your cabin, and your luggage should already be waiting for you there. Whether you've chosen an interior cabin, a river-view stateroom, or a luxurious suite, you'll find your accommodations to be thoughtfully designed and well-appointed.

Cabins on Rhone River cruise ships are typically compact but efficiently arranged to maximize space and comfort. Most cabins feature:

- Comfortable Beds: Often convertible between twin and queen configurations, with high-quality linens and pillows.
- En Suite Bathroom: Equipped with a shower, vanity, and premium toiletries. Some suites may include a bathtub.
- Storage Space: Closets, drawers, and under-bed storage for your luggage and personal belongings.
- Climate Control: Individual thermostats to ensure your comfort.
- Entertainment Options: Flat-screen TV with satellite channels, and often an infotainment system with movies and music.
- Balcony or Large Windows: Many cabins offer private balconies or floor-to-ceiling windows for unobstructed river views.
- Take some time to unpack and personalize your space. Having your belongings neatly organized will make your cabin feel like home for the duration of your cruise.

Exploring Onboard Amenities

Once you've settled into your cabin, take the opportunity to explore the ship at your own pace. Familiarize yourself with the locations of various amenities and facilities. Here are some highlights you won't want to miss:

- Dining Experiences: Beyond the main dining room, many ships feature specialty restaurants or al fresco dining options. Be sure to check the daily schedule for meal times and any special dining events.

- Bars and Lounges: Whether you prefer a quiet drink in an intimate setting or a lively bar with live music, you'll find a variety of options onboard. Most ships include a main bar in the lounge area and perhaps a more casual bar on the sun deck.
- Recreational Facilities: The fitness center is typically equipped with modern exercise machines, free weights, and space for yoga or stretching. The spa, if available, offers a range of treatments from massages to facials – a perfect way to unwind after a day of sightseeing.
- Entertainment and Activities: Check the daily program for a schedule of activities, which can include cooking demonstrations, wine tastings, lectures on local history and culture, and evening entertainment such as live music or performances by local artists.
- Boutiques and Shops: Some ships feature small shops where you can purchase souvenirs, local products, and essential items you might need during your cruise.

Meeting Fellow Passengers

One of the joys of river cruising is the opportunity to meet and interact with fellow travelers from around the world. The first evening onboard often includes a welcome reception or cocktail hour, where you can mingle with other passengers and meet the ship's officers and crew.

Dining is usually a social affair, with open seating encouraging guests to sit with different people at each meal. This fosters a sense of camaraderie and community, as you share stories and experiences with your fellow cruisers.

Preparing for the Journey Ahead

As you settle into your first evening onboard, take a moment to review the itinerary and plan your activities for the days ahead. Your cruise director will provide a detailed briefing on the upcoming ports of call, shore excursions, and onboard events. This is also a good time to ask any questions and make any necessary reservations for specialty dining or spa treatments.

The First Night Onboard

Dinner on the first night is often a highlight, featuring a special welcome menu that showcases the culinary expertise of the ship's chefs. Enjoy a leisurely meal, accompanied by fine wines and attentive service. After dinner, retire to the lounge for some light entertainment or simply relax on the sun deck, enjoying the serene river views under the stars.

2.2 Settling into Your Cabin: Comfort and Amenities

Your cabin will serve as your private retreat, offering a blend of modern amenities and cozy comfort. Here's an in-depth guide to understanding the different types of cabins, the amenities provided, and tips for making the most of your stay.

Types of Cabins

1. Interior Cabins

Interior cabins are a popular choice for budget-conscious travelers. These cabins, located in the interior of the ship, do not have windows or balconies, but they offer a cozy and efficient use of space. They are typically equipped with comfortable bedding, a private bathroom, and essential amenities such as a flat-screen TV and a safe for valuables. Despite the lack of a view, interior cabins are designed to be inviting and restful, making them a great option for those who plan to spend most of their time exploring the ship and destinations. Prices for interior cabins generally start at around $100 per night.

2. Oceanview Cabins

For those who prefer a view, oceanview cabins offer a window or porthole, providing natural light and a glimpse of the passing scenery. These cabins are slightly more expensive than interior cabins, with prices starting at around $150 per night. Oceanview cabins often feature similar amenities to interior cabins, including comfortable bedding, a private bathroom, and modern conveniences like a flat-screen TV and a mini-fridge. The window allows guests to enjoy the beautiful landscapes of the Rhone River without leaving the comfort of their cabin.

3. Balcony Cabins

Balcony cabins provide an elevated level of luxury, with private balconies offering stunning views of the river and surrounding landscapes. These cabins are ideal for travelers who enjoy relaxing in their private outdoor space, sipping a morning coffee, or unwinding with a glass of wine in the evening. Balcony cabins typically feature enhanced amenities such as larger living spaces, premium bedding, and additional seating. Prices for balcony cabins range from $200 to $500 per night, depending on the cruise line and itinerary.

4. Suites

For the ultimate in luxury and space, suites are the top choice. Suites offer expansive living areas, separate bedrooms, and large balconies with panoramic views. Guests in suites can enjoy a range of premium amenities, including plush bedding, spacious bathrooms with bathtubs, walk-in closets, and exclusive access to concierge services. Some suites even come with additional perks such as priority boarding, complimentary minibar, and private dining options. Prices for suites vary widely, starting at around $500 per night and going up to several thousand dollars per night for the most luxurious options.

Amenities in Your Cabin

1. Comfortable Bedding

A good night's sleep is essential for enjoying your cruise, and your cabin's bedding is designed to provide just that. Most cabins feature high-quality mattresses, soft pillows, and premium linens. If you have specific preferences, such as hypoallergenic bedding or extra pillows, don't hesitate to ask the housekeeping staff.

2. Private Bathroom

Your cabin includes a private bathroom equipped with a shower, toilet, and sink. Bathrooms are stocked with toiletries such as shampoo, conditioner, soap, and lotion. Some higher-end cabins and suites also feature bathtubs, double sinks, and luxury bath products. Housekeeping services ensure that your bathroom remains clean and well-stocked throughout your cruise.

3. Climate Control

To ensure your comfort, cabins are equipped with individual climate control systems. You can adjust the temperature to your liking, whether you prefer a cool retreat after a day of exploring or a warm haven during cooler evenings. The system is easy to use, and instructions are usually provided in the cabin.

4. Entertainment Options

Relaxing in your cabin is made easy with various entertainment options. Flat-screen TVs with a selection of channels and on-demand movies are standard in most cabins. Additionally, many cruise ships offer complimentary Wi-Fi, allowing you to stream your favorite shows, stay connected with loved ones, or plan your next day's activities. Check with your cruise line for Wi-Fi availability and pricing, as it can vary.

5. Storage Space

Efficient storage is essential for keeping your cabin organized. Most cabins feature ample closet space, drawers, and shelves for your belongings. Some cabins also include under-bed storage for suitcases. Utilize these spaces to keep your cabin tidy and maximize your living area.

6. Minibar and Room Service

Many cabins come with a minibar stocked with a selection of beverages and snacks. While some items may be complimentary, others may incur an additional charge, so be sure to check the pricing information provided in your cabin. Room service is also available, offering a range of food and drink options delivered directly to your cabin. Room service menus are typically available 24/7, allowing you to enjoy a meal or snack at any time.

7. Safety and Security

Your safety is a top priority, and your cabin is equipped with essential safety features. Each cabin has a safe for securing valuables such as passports, cash, and jewelry. Instructions for using the safe are provided, and it's a good idea to store your valuables there whenever you leave the cabin. In case of an emergency, familiarize yourself with the location of life jackets, which are typically stored in the closet, and review the emergency procedures outlined in the safety information provided in your cabin.

2.3 Meet the Crew: Your Guides and Staff Members

The Captain and Navigation Crew

At the helm of your Rhone River cruise ship is the captain, the master of the vessel. The captain's primary responsibility is to ensure the safe navigation of the ship along the Rhone River, a task that requires extensive experience and intimate knowledge of the river's currents, locks, and ports. On many cruises, the captain will make appearances during welcome and farewell events, offering passengers an opportunity to meet the individual responsible for their safe passage.

Supporting the captain is the navigation crew, including the first mate and other officers. These professionals work around the clock to monitor the ship's course, weather conditions, and any potential obstacles. They are highly trained and certified, often having years of experience navigating rivers and other waterways.

To engage with the captain and navigation crew, attend the ship's welcome reception or any scheduled meet-and-greet events. This is a great opportunity to ask questions about the ship, the river, and the navigation process. The captain's insights can enrich your understanding of the journey and highlight the complexities involved in river navigation.

Cruise Director and Entertainment Staff

The cruise director is the heartbeat of onboard entertainment and activities. This charismatic individual is responsible for organizing and overseeing all the social events, educational talks, and recreational activities that occur during the cruise. From daily briefings about upcoming ports of call to hosting themed parties and cultural performances, the cruise director ensures that there's always something engaging happening onboard.

Working closely with the cruise director is a team of entertainment staff, including performers, musicians, and activity coordinators. They bring the cruise to life with music, dance, and interactive games, providing passengers with a rich array of entertainment options.

Be sure to attend the daily briefings and activity announcements, usually held in the lounge or main hall. These sessions offer valuable information about the day's schedule and special events. Don't hesitate to introduce yourself to the cruise director and entertainment staff—they're always eager to meet passengers and welcome feedback about the entertainment offerings.

Shore Excursion Manager and Guides

One of the highlights of any Rhone River cruise is the shore excursions, and the shore excursion manager plays a pivotal role in organizing and coordinating these adventures. This individual works tirelessly to curate a selection of excursions that showcase the best of each destination along the Rhone, from historic walking tours in Avignon to wine tastings in Tain-l'Hermitage.

Accompanying you on these excursions are knowledgeable local guides who bring each destination to life with their expertise and passion. These guides often have deep roots in the region and can provide unique insights and stories that you won't find in any guidebook.

To get the most out of your shore excursions, attend the pre-excursion briefings where the shore excursion manager will outline the details of each tour, including what to bring, what to wear, and what to expect. During the excursions, take the opportunity to ask questions and engage with the local guides—they are a wealth of information and can offer personalized recommendations for exploring each destination.

Hospitality and Housekeeping Staff

The hospitality and housekeeping staff are the unsung heroes of your cruise experience, working behind the scenes to ensure that every aspect of your stay is comfortable and enjoyable. This dedicated team includes cabin stewards, cleaners, and laundry personnel who maintain the cleanliness and orderliness of your cabin and public areas.

Your cabin steward is often the most visible member of the housekeeping staff, responsible for daily cleaning and turndown service. They ensure that your cabin is always in top condition, providing fresh towels, replenishing toiletries, and addressing any special requests you might have.

To show appreciation for their hard work, consider leaving a small tip or a thank-you note for your cabin steward at the end of the cruise. While tipping policies vary by cruise line, a general guideline is $10 to $15 per day, which can be distributed among the housekeeping staff.

Dining and Culinary Team

One of the true pleasures of a Rhone River cruise is the culinary experience, and the dining and culinary team is at the heart of this gastronomic adventure. Led by the head chef, this team of skilled chefs and kitchen staff prepares a variety of delicious meals that highlight both international cuisine and regional specialties from the Rhone Valley.

The dining staff, including waiters and sommeliers, ensure that each meal is served with impeccable attention to detail. They can recommend the perfect wine pairing for your meal, accommodate dietary restrictions, and provide insights into the dishes being served.

To make the most of your dining experience, don't hesitate to ask the waitstaff for recommendations or to explain the ingredients and preparation methods of the dishes. If you have any dietary restrictions or special requests, inform the dining team at the beginning of your cruise so they can make the necessary arrangements.

Wellness and Spa Staff

For those seeking relaxation and rejuvenation, the wellness and spa staff are there to provide a range of services designed to pamper and refresh. From massage therapists and estheticians to fitness instructors and wellness coaches, this team offers a variety of treatments and activities to enhance your well-being.

Onboard spa services typically include massages, facials, manicures, and pedicures, with prices ranging from $50 for a basic treatment to $200 for more comprehensive packages. Fitness classes, such as yoga and Pilates, are often included in the cruise fare and provide a great way to stay active while enjoying the scenic views of the Rhone River.

To fully enjoy the wellness facilities, book your treatments early in the cruise as slots can fill up quickly. Attend the introductory wellness session to learn about the available services and to meet the wellness staff who can tailor treatments to your specific needs.

Engineering and Maintenance Crew

Behind the scenes, the engineering and maintenance crew work diligently to ensure the smooth operation of the ship. This team of skilled technicians is responsible for maintaining the ship's mechanical systems, plumbing, and electrical systems, ensuring that everything runs efficiently and safely.

While passengers rarely interact with the engineering and maintenance crew, their work is vital to the overall cruise experience. If you do encounter any technical issues in your cabin or elsewhere on the ship, report them promptly to the reception desk. The maintenance crew is always on hand to address any problems and ensure your comfort.

Reception and Guest Services

The reception and guest services team is your go-to resource for any questions, concerns, or special requests during your cruise. Located in the ship's main lobby, the reception desk is staffed 24/7 by friendly and knowledgeable personnel who can assist with everything from booking shore excursions to handling lost items.

The guest services team also coordinates communication between passengers and other departments, ensuring that any issues are resolved quickly and efficiently. Whether you need information about the day's activities, assistance with travel arrangements, or recommendations for exploring ports of call, the reception staff is there to help.

To make the most of their services, don't hesitate to visit the reception desk whenever you have a question or need assistance. They can provide maps, brochures, and detailed information about each destination, making them an invaluable resource throughout your cruise.

Medical Staff

While we hope you won't need their services, it's reassuring to know that a qualified medical team is onboard to handle any health issues that may arise. Most river cruise ships have a small medical facility staffed by a doctor and/or a nurse who can provide basic medical care and emergency services.

If you have any pre-existing medical conditions or require regular medication, inform the medical staff at the beginning of your cruise. This ensures they are prepared to assist you if needed. The medical facility is equipped to handle minor injuries and illnesses, but for more serious medical issues, arrangements can be made to visit a local hospital at the next port of call.

2.4 Safety First: Emergency Procedures and Precautions

While the scenic beauty and cultural experiences along the Rhone River are undoubtedly captivating, it's crucial to be prepared for any unexpected situations that may arise. In this section, we'll delve deeper into the importance of safety onboard your cruise ship, highlighting emergency procedures and precautions to ensure a smooth and secure journey.

Understanding Emergency Procedures

Your cruise ship is equipped with comprehensive safety measures and protocols to handle a wide range of emergency scenarios. Before setting sail, familiarize yourself with the ship's layout, including the location of emergency exits, life jackets, and muster stations. These vital components are clearly marked throughout the ship and detailed in the safety information provided in your cabin.

In the event of an emergency, such as a fire, collision, or adverse weather conditions, the crew is trained to swiftly respond and guide passengers to safety. Regular safety drills are conducted to ensure that both passengers and crew members are prepared to handle emergencies effectively. During these drills, you'll receive detailed instructions on evacuation procedures and muster station locations, so it's essential to participate attentively.

Safety Equipment and Resources

Your safety onboard is supported by a range of essential equipment and resources designed to mitigate risks and ensure swift response to emergencies. Life jackets are readily available in your cabin and designated muster stations, and it's imperative to familiarize yourself with their proper use. In the event of a water evacuation, wearing a life jacket can significantly increase your chances of survival.

Additionally, the ship is equipped with firefighting equipment, emergency lighting, and communication systems to facilitate prompt response and coordination during emergencies. Crew members undergo rigorous training to operate this equipment effectively and maintain a safe environment for all passengers.

Safety Precautions for Passengers

While the crew is responsible for managing emergency situations and ensuring passenger safety, there are several precautions that passengers can take to minimize risks and contribute to a safe cruising experience:

- Stay Informed: Pay attention to safety announcements and instructions provided by the captain and crew. These may include updates on weather conditions, safety procedures, and emergency protocols. Remain vigilant and alert to any changes or developments during your cruise.
- Buddy System: Traveling with a companion is not only enjoyable but also enhances safety. Establish a buddy system with your travel partner or group members to ensure that everyone stays together and accounted for in the event of an emergency.
- Personal Responsibility: Take responsibility for your own safety by following safety guidelines and regulations. Avoid engaging in risky behavior or disregarding safety instructions, as this could jeopardize your well-being and that of others onboard.
- Stay Sober: While it's tempting to indulge in the onboard amenities, including alcoholic beverages, it's essential to drink responsibly. Excessive alcohol consumption can impair judgment and coordination, increasing the risk of accidents and injuries. If you choose to drink alcohol, do so in moderation and be mindful of your limits.
- Be Mindful of Your Surroundings: Pay attention to your surroundings and exercise caution when moving around the ship, especially in areas such as staircases, decks, and pool areas. Watch for wet or slippery surfaces and use handrails when necessary to prevent slips and falls.
- Emergency Contacts and Medical Assistance: Familiarize yourself with the ship's medical facilities

and procedures for accessing medical assistance in case of illness or injury. Keep essential medications and medical supplies readily accessible in your cabin, and notify the ship's medical staff if you require assistance.

CHAPTER THREE
EXPLORING RHONE RIVER PORTS OF CALL

3.1 Lyon: The Gastronomic Capital of France

3.1.1 Must-Visit Attractions: From Old Town to the Basilica of Notre-Dame de Fourvière

As you embark on your Rhone River cruise, Lyon serves as a captivating starting point with its blend of ancient and modern attractions. This chapter guides you through the must-visit sites, from the charming Old Town to the awe-inspiring Basilica of Notre-Dame de Fourvière, ensuring you make the most of your time in this vibrant city.

1. Vieux Lyon: A Journey Back in Time

Begin your exploration in Vieux Lyon, the city's Old Town, a UNESCO World Heritage site that transports you back to the Renaissance era. This area, one of the largest Renaissance districts in Europe, is a labyrinth of narrow, cobblestone streets, hidden courtyards, and pastel-colored buildings adorned with ornate facades.

Start at the Place Saint-Jean, the heart of Vieux Lyon, where you'll find the magnificent Cathédrale Saint-Jean-Baptiste. This Gothic and Romanesque cathedral, dating back to the 12th century, is renowned for its stunning astronomical clock, which has been in operation since the 14th century. The cathedral is open daily from 8 AM to 7 PM, and entry is free. Don't miss the chance to attend a mass or a choral performance to experience the cathedral's acoustics and spiritual ambiance.

As you wander through the Old Town, explore the Traboules—hidden passageways that connect buildings through courtyards and spiral staircases. Originally used by silk merchants to transport their goods, these passageways offer a unique glimpse into Lyon's past. Some of the best-preserved traboules can be found along Rue Saint-Jean and Rue du Bœuf. While many traboules are private, a number are open to the public. Look for signs indicating public access, and enjoy the adventure of uncovering these secret pathways.

2. The Basilica of Notre-Dame de Fourvière: Panoramic Splendor

Perched atop Fourvière Hill, the Basilica of Notre-Dame de Fourvière is one of Lyon's most iconic landmarks. Constructed in the late 19th century, this basilica is a blend of Romanesque and Byzantine architecture, featuring intricate mosaics, stunning stained glass windows, and a richly decorated interior.

To reach the basilica, you can take the funicular from Vieux Lyon, which operates daily from 6 AM to midnight. The ride costs around $3, offering a quick and scenic ascent up the hill. Alternatively, if you're feeling adventurous, you can hike up the hill via the Montée des Chazeaux, a picturesque path that rewards you with breathtaking views of the city along the way.

The basilica is open daily from 8 AM to 7 PM, and entry is free, although donations are welcome. Inside, marvel at the exquisite mosaics depicting scenes from the Virgin Mary's life, and take a moment to appreciate the peaceful atmosphere. For a small fee of around $3, you can visit the basilica's crypt, dedicated to Saint Joseph, which features a serene chapel and beautiful sculptures.

One of the highlights of visiting the basilica is the panoramic view from the esplanade. On a clear day, you can see the entire city of Lyon, with its red-tiled roofs, historic buildings, and the winding Rhône and Saône rivers. The view extends to the Alps in the distance, making it a perfect spot for photography.

Adjacent to the basilica is the Fourvière Museum, which provides insight into the basilica's history and construction. The museum is open Tuesday to Sunday, 10 AM to 6 PM, with an entry fee of around $5. Here, you can explore exhibits featuring religious artifacts, architectural models, and historical photographs, deepening your understanding of this significant site.

3. Ancient Theatre of Fourvière: A Glimpse into Roman Lyon

Just below the basilica lies the Ancient Theatre of Fourvière, a remarkable remnant of Roman Lyon. Built in 15 BC, this theatre could originally seat up to 10,000 spectators and hosted various performances and public gatherings. Today, it is one of the best-preserved Roman theatres in France and continues to serve as a cultural venue.

During the summer, the theatre comes alive with the Nuits de Fourvière festival, which runs from June to August. This festival features a diverse array of performances, including music, dance, theatre, and cinema. Tickets for the festival range from $30 to $150, depending on the event and seating. Attending a performance in this ancient setting is a truly magical experience, blending history and contemporary culture.

The theatre is open to visitors year-round, and admission is free. As you walk through the ruins, imagine the grandeur of Roman spectacles and the vibrant life of ancient Lyon. The site also includes the Odéon, a smaller theatre used for musical performances, and the Museum of Gallo-Roman Civilization, located nearby at 17 Rue Cléberg. The museum, open Wednesday to Monday, 10 AM to 6 PM, with an entry fee of $7, houses an impressive collection of artifacts from the Roman period, including mosaics, sculptures, and everyday objects.

4. Musée Gadagne: Lyon's History and Puppetry Arts

For a comprehensive understanding of Lyon's history, visit the Musée Gadagne, located at 1 Place du Petit Collège in Vieux Lyon. This museum complex, housed in a beautifully restored Renaissance building, comprises the Museum of History of Lyon and the Museum of Puppetry Arts.

The Museum of History of Lyon takes you through the city's rich past, from its founding by the Romans to its role as a major silk production center in the 19th century. The museum's exhibits include historical maps, paintings, and artifacts, providing a detailed narrative of Lyon's evolution. The museum is open Wednesday to Sunday, 11 AM to 6:30 PM, with an admission fee of $9.

The Museum of Puppetry Arts showcases Lyon's unique contribution to the world of puppetry, featuring an extensive collection of puppets from around the globe. The highlight of the museum is the Guignol puppets, a traditional Lyonnais puppet show that originated in the early 19th century. Interactive exhibits and live puppet performances make this museum a delight for visitors of all ages.

5. Place Bellecour: The Heart of Lyon

After exploring the historic sites, make your way to Place Bellecour, the largest open square in Lyon and one of the largest in Europe. This vast, pedestrian-friendly square is a central hub, surrounded by shops, cafes, and historic buildings. In the center of the square stands an equestrian statue of King Louis XIV, a prominent landmark.

Place Bellecour is an ideal spot to relax and people-watch, especially in the warmer months when the square comes alive with street performers and events. The Tourist Information Office, located at the southern end of the square, is a great resource for maps, brochures, and personalized advice on exploring Lyon.

From Place Bellecour, you can easily access Lyon's main shopping streets, Rue de la République and Rue Victor Hugo, both lined with a mix of high-end boutiques, international brands, and local shops. This area is perfect for a leisurely stroll and some retail therapy.

6. Presqu'île: The Cultural and Commercial Heart

The Presqu'île district, a narrow strip of land between the Rhône and Saône rivers, is the cultural and commercial heart of Lyon. Start your exploration at Place des Terreaux, home to the majestic Hôtel de Ville (City Hall) and the Musée des Beaux-Arts. The museum, located at 20 Place des Terreaux, is one of the finest art museums in France, boasting an extensive collection that spans from ancient Egypt to contemporary art. The museum is open Wednesday to Monday, 10 AM to 6 PM, with an admission fee of $10.

Continue your journey along Rue de la République, Lyon's main shopping street, which leads to the Place de la République and Place des Jacobins. Here, you'll find a variety of shops, cafes, and restaurants, offering everything from high fashion to local delicacies.

For a taste of Lyon's vibrant nightlife, head to Rue Mercière, a bustling street lined with bars, bistros, and restaurants.

This area comes alive in the evening, offering a lively atmosphere and a wide range of dining options, from traditional Lyonnais cuisine to international flavors.

7. Parc de la Tête d'Or: A Green Oasis in the City

When you need a break from the hustle and bustle of the city, escape to Parc de la Tête d'Or, one of Europe's largest urban parks. Located in the 6th arrondissement, this 290-acre park offers a serene retreat with its beautiful gardens, expansive lawns, and a large lake.

The park is open daily from 6:30 AM to 10:30 PM and entry is free. Stroll through the Botanical Garden, home to over 15,000 plant species, or visit the free zoo, which houses a variety of animals, including giraffes, deer, and flamingos. Rent a paddleboat for a leisurely ride on the lake, or simply relax with a picnic on the grass.

For families, the park offers several attractions, including a small amusement park, a miniature train, and pony rides. There's also a rose garden with over 30,000 rose bushes, providing a colorful and fragrant experience, especially in the spring and summer.

8. Les Halles de Lyon Paul Bocuse: A Food Lover's Paradise

No visit to Lyon would be complete without experiencing its culinary delights, and there's no better place to start than Les Halles de Lyon Paul Bocuse. This indoor market, named after the legendary chef Paul Bocuse, is a food lover's paradise, offering a wide range of gourmet products, from cheesesand charcuterie to pastries and chocolates.

Located at 102 Cours Lafayette, Les Halles de Lyon is open from Tuesday to Sunday, 7 AM to 10:30 PM. As you wander through the market, you'll encounter an array of stalls and vendors showcasing the finest produce and specialties from the Lyon region and beyond. Take your time to sample local cheeses from La Mère Richard, indulge in artisanal chocolates from Sève, or pick up a selection of cured meats from Colette Sibilia.

For a true taste of Lyonnais cuisine, head to one of the market's eateries, where you can enjoy classic dishes like quenelles, coq au vin, and boudin noir. Le Comptoir du Marché, located within Les Halles, offers a variety of dishes prepared with fresh market ingredients, with prices ranging from $20 to $50 per person.

3.1.2 Culinary Delights: Sampling Lyon's Famous Cuisine

Les Halles de Lyon Paul Bocuse

Begin your culinary adventure at Les Halles de Lyon Paul Bocuse, an indoor market named after the legendary chef Paul Bocuse. Located at 102 Cours Lafayette, this market is a treasure trove of gourmet foods and local delicacies. Open from Tuesday to Sunday, 7 AM to 10:30 PM, it's the perfect place to immerse yourself in the flavors of Lyon.

As you wander through the market, you'll find over 50 stalls offering everything from cheeses and charcuterie to seafood and pastries. Be sure to visit La Mère Richard for a taste of their famous Saint-Marcellin cheese, a creamy delight that melts in your mouth. A typical cheese platter here costs around $15.

For charcuterie, Colette Sibilia is a must-visit. Sample the saucisson sec, a dry-cured sausage that pairs perfectly with a glass of local wine. A charcuterie board will set you back around $20. If you have a sweet tooth, stop by Sève for exquisite chocolates and pralines, with prices starting at $10 for a small selection.

Many of the market's vendors offer tasting portions, allowing you to sample a wide range of products without committing to a full purchase. Plan to spend at least a couple of hours here, savoring the sights, smells, and tastes of Lyon's culinary heart.

Bouchons Lyonnais

To truly experience Lyon's culinary traditions, a visit to a bouchon is essential. These small, family-run eateries are known for their hearty, rustic dishes that have been passed down through generations. One of the most popular bouchons is Le Café des Fédérations, located at 8 Rue Major Martin.

Le Café des Fédérations offers a fixed-price menu for around $35 per person, which includes several courses of traditional Lyonnaise dishes. Start with a salad lyonnaise, a robust salad featuring frisée lettuce, bacon, poached eggs, and croutons. Follow this with quenelles de brochet, light and airy pike fish dumplings served with a rich crayfish sauce.

Andouillette, a type of tripe sausage, is another local specialty worth trying. Its strong flavor might not be for everyone, but it's a quintessential part of Lyon's culinary heritage. End your meal with a slice of tarte aux pralines, a bright pink tart made with almond pralines. The warm, friendly atmosphere of the bouchon, combined with the delicious food, makes for an unforgettable dining experience.

Fine Dining: L'Auberge du Pont de Collonges

For those seeking a more upscale dining experience, L'Auberge du Pont de Collonges, Paul Bocuse's three-

Michelin-star restaurant, is a must-visit. Located at 40 Rue de la Plage in Collonges-au-Mont-d'Or, this restaurant has been a temple of haute cuisine for decades. Open Tuesday to Saturday, with lunch served from 12 PM to 1:30 PM and dinner from 7:30 PM to 9:30 PM, it offers a luxurious setting for a special meal.

A typical tasting menu here starts at $250 per person, featuring a selection of Bocuse's signature dishes. Begin with the famous Soupe aux truffes V.G.E., a truffle soup encased in a puff pastry dome, created for a presidential dinner in 1975. Follow this with the Bresse chicken in a bladder, a visually stunning and exquisitely flavored dish.

The dining experience at L'Auberge du Pont de Collonges is as much about the presentation and service as it is about the food. Each dish is meticulously crafted and beautifully presented, ensuring that your meal is a feast for both the eyes and the palate. Be sure to book well in advance, as tables at this iconic restaurant are highly sought after.

Food Tours and Cooking Classes

To gain a deeper understanding of Lyon's culinary culture, consider joining a food tour or taking a cooking class. The Original Food Tour Lyon offers guided tours that take you through the city's markets, bouchons, and specialty food shops. Prices for these tours start at $75 per person and include numerous tastings.

Alternatively, enroll in a cooking class at L'Atelier des Sens, located at 31 Rue Casimir Périer. Here, you can learn to prepare classic Lyonnaise dishes under the guidance of professional chefs. Classes range from $100 to $150 per person, depending on the length and complexity of the course. It's a hands-on way to bring a piece of Lyon's culinary magic back home with you.

1. Local Markets

Lyon's markets are an integral part of its culinary scene, offering fresh, local produce and artisanal products. In addition to Les Halles de Lyon Paul Bocuse, several outdoor markets are worth visiting. The Marché de la Croix-Rousse, held daily except Monday on Boulevard de la Croix-Rousse, is a vibrant market where you can find everything from fresh fruits and vegetables to flowers and crafts.

Another notable market is the Marché Saint-Antoine Célestins, located along the banks of the Saône River. Open every morning except Monday, this market is known for its high-quality produce and specialty food items. Spend around $20 to $30 here on a selection of fresh bread, cheese, and charcuterie for a perfect picnic by the river.

2. Wine Tasting

Lyon's proximity to some of France's most prestigious wine regions, including Beaujolais and the Northern Rhône Valley, makes it an excellent base for wine tasting. Many local wine bars and cellars offer tastings and wine education sessions.

Le Vercoquin, located at 33 Rue de la Martinière, is a cozy wine bar offering an extensive selection of wines by the glass. Prices range from $5 to $15 per glass, and the knowledgeable staff can help you choose the perfect wine to suit your palate.

For a more immersive experience, consider a half-day wine tour with Rhône Trip. These tours take you to local vineyards and wineries, where you can learn about the wine-making process and sample some exceptional wines. Prices start at $90 per person, and the tours typically include transportation, tastings, and a guided tour of the vineyards.

3. Sweet Treats

Lyon is also famous for its pastries and desserts. Don't miss the chance to try some of the city's sweet delights, such as the iconic praline tart. Maison Pralus, located at 32 Rue de Brest, is renowned for its praluline, a brioche filled with pink pralines. A small praluline costs around $8, and it makes for a delicious snack or souvenir.

For a classic French pastry experience, visit Pâtisserie Sève at 29 Quai Saint-Antoine. This bakery offers an array of beautifully crafted pastries, from éclairs and macarons to tarts and cakes. Prices range from $3 to $7 per pastry, and each bite is a testament to the skill and creativity of Lyon's pastry chefs.

4. Street Food

Lyon's street food scene is a delightful mix of traditional and modern flavors. Head to the Food Traboule, a food hall located at 22 Rue du Bœuf, which brings together some of Lyon's best street food vendors under one roof. Open daily from 11 AM to 10 PM, it's a great place to sample a variety of dishes in a casual, vibrant setting.

At Food Traboule, you can try everything from gourmet burgers and wood-fired pizzas to innovative fusion dishes and classic French fare. Prices vary by vendor, but you can expect to spend around $15 to $25 for a meal. The lively atmosphere and diverse food options make it a popular spot for both locals and tourists.

3.1.3 Shopping and Strolling: Markets, Boutiques, and Quaint Streets

The Presqu'île District: The Heart of Lyon's Shopping Scene

The Presqu'île district, located between the Rhône and Saône rivers, is the epicenter of Lyon's shopping experience. This area is home to an array of high-end boutiques, department stores, and local shops. Start your shopping adventure on Rue de la République, one of Lyon's main shopping streets. Here, you'll find major brands like Galeries Lafayette (42 Boulevard Haussmann, open Monday to Saturday from 9:30 AM to 8 PM), which offers a wide range of fashion, beauty, and home goods.

Just a short walk away, Rue du Président Édouard Herriot is another shopping haven, featuring luxury boutiques such as Louis Vuitton (70 Rue du Président Édouard Herriot, open Monday to Saturday from 10 AM to 7 PM) and Hermès (48 Rue du Président Édouard Herriot, open Monday to Saturday from 10 AM to 7 PM). Whether you're looking to splurge on designer goods or simply window shop, this district provides a taste of luxury in Lyon.

For a more eclectic shopping experience, head to Rue de Brest and Rue Mercière, where you'll find a mix of trendy shops, bookstores, and cafes. This area is perfect for a leisurely afternoon of shopping and people-watching, with plenty of opportunities to stop for a coffee or a glass of wine at one of the many sidewalk cafes.

Village des Créateurs: Showcasing Local Talent

Located in the Passage Thiaffait, the Village des Créateurs is a creative hub that showcases the works of local designers and artisans. This passage is a hidden gem, offering unique fashion, jewelry, and home décor items. The shops here are open Monday to Saturday from 10 AM to 7 PM, and browsing through the creations of Lyon's talented designers is a delightful experience.

Passage Thiaffait itself is an architectural marvel, with its glass-covered walkways and elegant design. It's a perfect spot for discovering one-of-a-kind pieces that you won't find anywhere else. Whether you're looking for a statement piece of jewelry or a unique souvenir, the Village des Créateurs offers a diverse range of high-quality items.

Croix-Rousse: A Bohemian Vibe

The Croix-Rousse district, known for its bohemian vibe and artistic flair, is a must-visit for those who appreciate a more laid-back and creative atmosphere. Start your visit at the Marché de la Croix-Rousse, an open-air market held daily except Monday on Boulevard de la Croix-Rousse. This market is a feast for the senses, offering fresh produce, local cheeses, charcuterie, and handmade crafts. It's an excellent place to pick up unique souvenirs and enjoy the lively atmosphere. Expect to spend around $20 to $40 on local goodies.

After exploring the market, take a stroll through the surrounding streets, where you'll find independent boutiques, vintage shops, and artisan workshops. La Fromagerie du Vieux Lyon (58 Rue Saint-Jean, open Tuesday to Sunday from 9 AM to 7 PM) is a highlight, offering a wide variety of local cheeses that are perfect for a picnic or a gift.

Don't miss the Mur des Canuts, a massive mural that celebrates the history of the silk workers who once lived and worked in this area. The mural is located at 36 Boulevard des Canuts and is a stunning example of Lyon's commitment to preserving its cultural heritage.

Vieux Lyon: Stepping Back in Time

Vieux Lyon, the city's Old Town, is a UNESCO World Heritage site that offers a charming blend of history and shopping. Wander through its narrow, cobblestone streets, and you'll discover a treasure trove of boutiques, antique shops, and artisan stores. Rue Saint-Jean and Rue du Bœuf are particularly noteworthy, lined with shops selling handmade crafts, antiques, and souvenirs.

For a truly unique shopping experience, visit the Traboules, hidden passageways that were originally used by silk merchants. These passageways provide shortcuts through the city's medieval buildings and are a fascinating way to explore Vieux Lyon's history. Many of the Traboules are open to the public, and you can access them from streets like Rue Saint-Jean and Rue du Bœuf.

One of the highlights of Vieux Lyon is the Musée Miniature et Cinéma (60 Rue Saint-Jean, open every day from 10 AM to 6:30 PM, admission fee $12), which showcases miniature scenes and props from famous films. The museum shop offers unique movie memorabilia and miniature replicas that make for perfect souvenirs.

Confluence: Modern Shopping in a Trendy Setting

The Confluence district, located at the meeting point of the Rhône and Saône rivers, is a modern, trendy area that has become one of Lyon's most popular shopping destinations. The centerpiece of this district is the Confluence shopping center (112 Cours Charlemagne, open Monday to Saturday from 10 AM to 8 PM), a sleek, contemporary mall that features a wide range of shops, from international brands to local boutiques.

The Confluence district is also home to the Marché du Quai Saint-Antoine, a riverside market held every Sunday from 8 AM to 1 PM. This market offers fresh produce, flowers, and local specialties, making it a great place to shop for a picnic or to enjoy a leisurely stroll along the river.

For a unique shopping experience, visit the rooftop garden of the Confluence shopping center, which offers stunning views of the city and the rivers. The rooftop is open during the shopping center's hours and provides a relaxing escape from the hustle and bustle of the city.

Practical Tips for Shopping in Lyon

When shopping in Lyon, it's helpful to keep a few practical tips in mind:

- Opening Hours: Most shops in Lyon are open from 10 AM to 7 PM, Monday to Saturday. Markets typically start early, around 7 AM, and close by 1 PM. On Sundays, many shops are closed, but some markets and boutiques in tourist areas remain open.
- Payment: Credit cards are widely accepted, but it's always a good idea to carry some cash, especially when shopping at markets and smaller boutiques.
- Tax-Free Shopping: Non-EU residents can take advantage of tax-free shopping on purchases over

€100. Look for shops displaying the Tax-Free Shopping logo and don't forget to ask for your refund form at the point of purchase.

- Packing: If you plan on buying delicate items like wine or cheese, consider bringing bubble wrap or a padded bag to protect your purchases during travel.

Making the Most of Your Strolls

Lyon is a city best explored on foot, and taking the time to stroll through its various districts will reward you with countless discoveries. Here are some tips to enhance your strolling experience:

- Comfortable Footwear: Lyon's cobblestone streets and hilly terrain require comfortable walking shoes. Make sure to wear shoes that provide good support, especially if you plan on exploring areas like Vieux Lyon and Croix-Rousse.
- Weather Preparation: Lyon has a temperate climate, but it's always wise to check the weather forecast before heading out. Carrying an umbrella or a light jacket can help you stay comfortable during unexpected weather changes.
- Guided Tours: Consider joining a guided walking tour to learn more about Lyon's history and culture. Many tours focus on specific themes, such as food, architecture, or history, providing deeper insights into the city. Prices for guided tours typically range from $20 to $50 per person.
- Picnic Spots: Lyon has numerous parks and green spaces perfect for a relaxing picnic. Parc de la Tête d'Or, located in the 6th arrondissement, is one of the largest urban parks in France and offers beautiful

gardens, a lake, and even a small zoo. It's an ideal spot to unwind and enjoy your market purchases.

- Photography: Lyon's picturesque streets and historic buildings offer endless photo opportunities. Don't forget your camera or smartphone to capture the charming scenes you'll encounter during your strolls.

Beyond Shopping: Enjoying Lyon's Cafes and Bistros

Part of the charm of shopping and strolling in Lyon is taking breaks at the city's many cafes and bistros. These establishments offer a chance to relax, people-watch, and sample local delicacies. Here are a few recommendations:

- Le Café du Soleil (2 Place du Gouvernement, open Monday to Sunday from 8 AM to 11 PM): Located in Vieux Lyon, this charming cafe serves traditional Lyonnaise dishes and offers outdoor seating perfect for a sunny day.
- Boulangerie du Palais (8 Rue du Palais de Justice, open Tuesday to Sunday from 7 AM to 8 PM): A must-visit for pastry lovers, this bakery offers delicious croissants, tarts, and other baked goods that are perfect for a mid-morning snack.
- Café Comptoir Abel (25 Rue Guynemer, open Monday to Saturday from 12 PM to 2:30 PM and 7 PM to 10:30 PM): One of the oldest bistros in Lyon, it serves classic dishes in a cozy, nostalgic setting. It's an excellent spot for a leisurely lunch or dinner.
- Le Sucre (50 Quai Rambaud, open Tuesday to Sunday from 12 PM to 12 AM): This rooftop bar offers stunning views of Lyon's skyline and the river. It's the

perfect place to enjoy a cocktail or a glass of wine as you watch the sun set over the city.

- Le Comptoir de la Bourse (1 Place des Cordeliers, open Monday to Saturday from 7:30 AM to 11 PM): Located near the Lyon Stock Exchange, this cafe is known for its delicious coffee and pastries. It's a great spot for a quick caffeine fix or a leisurely breakfast.
- La Boîte à Café (3 Rue de la Baleine, open Monday to Friday from 8 AM to 7 PM and Saturday from 9 AM to 7 PM): This cozy cafe is a favorite among locals for its friendly atmosphere and excellent coffee. It's a perfect place to recharge during your shopping adventures.
- Le Kitchen Café (34 Rue Chevreul, open Tuesday to Sunday from 9 AM to 6 PM): This charming cafe offers a delicious brunch menu featuring fresh, locally sourced ingredients. It's a popular spot, so be sure to arrive early to snag a table.
- Le Jardin des Chartreux (32 Rue des Tables Claudiennes, open Tuesday to Sunday from 12 PM to 2 PM and 7:30 PM to 10 PM): Tucked away in a peaceful courtyard, this restaurant offers seasonal dishes made with ingredients from local farmers and producers. It's a hidden gem that's worth seeking out.

3.1.4 Cultural Gems: Museums, Galleries, and Theaters

Museums in Lyon

1. Musée des Beaux-Arts (Fine Arts Museum)

Located at 20 Place des Terreaux, the Musée des Beaux-Arts is housed in a 17th-century former convent and is often referred to as the "Little Louvre." The museum's extensive collection spans from antiquity to modern art, making it one of the most important art museums in France. Highlights include works by masters such as Rubens, Rembrandt, Poussin, and Delacroix, as well as an impressive collection of Impressionist and Modernist art featuring artists like Monet, Van Gogh, and Picasso.

- Opening Hours: Wednesday to Monday, 10 AM to 6 PM; closed on Tuesdays.
- Admission: $10 for adults, free for children under 18.
- Tips: To make the most of your visit, consider joining a guided tour, available for an additional $5. The museum also has a lovely café and a bookshop for art-related souvenirs.

2. Musée d'Art Contemporain de Lyon (Museum of Contemporary Art)

Situated in the Cité Internationale district, this museum is dedicated to contemporary art from the 1960s to the present. The Musée d'Art Contemporain hosts rotating exhibitions featuring international and French artists, making each visit unique. The building itself, designed by Renzo Piano, is a modern architectural masterpiece.

- Opening Hours: Wednesday to Sunday, 11 AM to 6 PM.
- Admission: $8 for adults, free for students and under 18s.
- Tips: Check the museum's website for current exhibitions and special events. Don't miss the rooftop terrace for a unique view of the city.

3. Musée Gadagne (Gadagne Museums)

Located at 1 Place du Petit Collège, the Musée Gadagne comprises two museums: the Museum of History of Lyon and the Museum of Puppetry Arts. The former explores the city's history from ancient times to the present, while the latter celebrates the art of puppetry with a focus on Lyon's famous Guignol puppet.

- Opening Hours: Wednesday to Sunday, 11 AM to 6:30 PM.
- Admission: $9 for adults, free for children under 18.
- Tips: Allow at least two hours to explore both museums thoroughly. The building's Renaissance architecture and tranquil courtyard garden are attractions in their own right.

4. Institut Lumière

At 25 Rue du Premier Film, the Institut Lumière is a museum dedicated to the Lumière brothers, pioneers of cinema who invented the Cinématographe. The museum is located in their family home and includes the original equipment used to create the first films, as well as a cinema that screens classic films.

- Opening Hours: Tuesday to Sunday, 10 AM to 6:30 PM.
- Admission: $7 for adults, free for children under 18.
- Tips: Film enthusiasts should not miss the daily screenings. The museum shop offers a range of film-related memorabilia.

Art Galleries in Lyon

1. Galerie Le Réverbère

Located at 38 Rue Burdeau, Galerie Le Réverbère is one of Lyon's premier contemporary art galleries, specializing in photography. The gallery represents both established and emerging artists and is known for its innovative and thought-provoking exhibitions.

- Opening Hours: Wednesday to Saturday, 2 PM to 7 PM.
- Admission: Free.
- Tips: Visit during an opening night to experience the vibrant local art scene and possibly meet the artists.

2. Galerie Estades

This gallery, at 61 Quai St Vincent, focuses on 20th-century French painting and sculpture, featuring artists such as Bernard Buffet and André Cottavoz. It's an excellent place to appreciate and purchase fine art.

- Opening Hours: Tuesday to Saturday, 10 AM to 12 PM and 2 PM to 7 PM.
- Admission: Free.
- Tips: The knowledgeable staff are passionate about art and can provide detailed information on the works and artists.

Theaters in Lyon

1. Opéra de Lyon (Lyon Opera House)

The Opéra de Lyon, located at 1 Place de la Comédie, is a stunning blend of classical and modern architecture. The original 1831 building was redesigned in 1993 by Jean Nouvel, who added a striking glass dome. The opera house hosts a diverse program of opera, ballet, and concerts throughout the year.

- Performances: Vary by season; check the website for current schedule.
- Tickets: $20 to $150, depending on the performance and seat selection.
- Tips: Book tickets in advance, especially for popular shows. Consider taking a backstage tour for a behind-the-scenes look at this magnificent venue.

2. Théâtre des Célestins

Situated at 4 Rue Charles Dullin, this historic theater has been a cultural landmark in Lyon since the 18th century. The Théâtre des Célestins presents a wide range of performances, including classic and contemporary plays, as well as dance and music.

- Performances: Vary by season; check the website for current schedule.
- Tickets: $15 to $80, depending on the performance and seat selection.
- Tips: Arrive early to admire the theater's ornate interior and enjoy a drink at the foyer bar.

3. Les Subsistances

Located at 8 bis Quai Saint-Vincent, Les Subsistances is a multidisciplinary cultural center housed in a former convent. It's known for its innovative and avant-garde performances in theater, dance, and visual arts.

- Performances: Vary by season; check the website for current schedule.
- Tickets: $10 to $50, depending on the performance.
- Tips: This venue often hosts experimental and contemporary works, making it a great place to discover cutting-edge art.

Practical Tips for Visiting Cultural Attractions in Lyon

- Timing: Most museums and galleries are closed on Mondays and major holidays. Plan your visits accordingly to avoid disappointment.
- Tickets: Consider purchasing a Lyon City Card, which provides free or discounted entry to many museums, guided tours, and public transportation. The card costs $30 for 24 hours, $45 for 48 hours, and $60 for 72 hours.
- Guided Tours: Many museums offer guided tours in English, which can enhance your understanding and appreciation of the exhibits. Check the museum websites for tour schedules and prices.
- Photography: While most museums allow photography without flash, some special exhibitions may have restrictions. Always check the museum's policy before taking pictures.
- Accessibility: Lyon's major cultural attractions are generally accessible to visitors with disabilities. If you have specific needs, contact the venue in advance to ensure a smooth visit.
- Cafés and Shops: Many museums have excellent cafés and gift shops. Take the time to relax with a coffee and browse for unique souvenirs.

3.2 Vienne: A Journey Through Roman History

Vienne, nestled along the banks of the Rhone River, offers a captivating journey through Roman history and contemporary charm. As you step ashore, prepare to immerse yourself in a tapestry of ancient ruins, cultural treasures, and gastronomic delights.

3.2.1 Landmarks and Ruins: Discovering Ancient Vienne

1. Temple of Augustus and Livia

The Temple of Augustus and Livia is one of Vienne's most iconic landmarks, standing as a testament to the architectural prowess of the Roman Empire. Constructed in the early 1st century BC, this Corinthian-style temple was dedicated to Emperor Augustus and his wife, Livia. Its impressive façade, adorned with fluted columns and intricate friezes, offers a glimpse into the grandeur of Roman religious architecture.

Visitors can explore the temple's exterior, where detailed carvings depict scenes from Roman mythology and daily life. The temple's central location in Vienne makes it easily accessible, and it's a perfect starting point for a historical tour of the town. The temple is open daily from 9:00 AM to 6:00 PM, and admission is free, allowing visitors to immerse themselves in the ancient ambiance without any cost.

2. Roman Theater

A short walk from the Temple of Augustus and Livia brings you to the Roman Theater, one of the largest and best-preserved Roman theaters in Europe. Built into the hillside in the early 1st century AD, this amphitheater could accommodate up to 13,000 spectators, who gathered to watch plays, musical performances, and gladiatorial contests.

Today, the theater is a vibrant cultural venue, hosting events such as the annual Jazz à Vienne festival, which attracts artists and audiences from around the world. Guided tours are available, offering detailed insights into the theater's history and architecture. The theater is open daily from 9:00 AM to 7:00 PM, with an admission fee of $10 per person.

3. Garden of Cybele

Adjacent to the Roman Theater is the Garden of Cybele, a tranquil green space that serves as an oasis of calm in the heart of Vienne. This garden is named after Cybele, an ancient Phrygian goddess of fertility and nature, whose cult was popular in the Roman Empire. The garden features several Roman-era sculptures, including statues and altars dedicated to Cybele.

As you stroll through the garden, you can admire the remnants of Roman buildings, including fragments of columns and stone inscriptions. The garden's serene atmosphere, combined with its historical significance, makes it a perfect spot for relaxation and reflection. The Garden of Cybele is open daily from dawn to dusk, and admission is free.

4. Gallo-Roman Museum of Saint-Romain-en-Gal

To delve deeper into Vienne's Roman heritage, a visit to the Gallo-Roman Museum of Saint-Romain-en-Gal is essential. Located just across the river from Vienne, this museum and archaeological site cover over 7 hectares, showcasing the remains of a thriving Roman settlement. The museum's exhibits include an extensive collection of mosaics, pottery, sculptures, and everyday objects that provide a comprehensive overview of life in Roman Gaul.

Visitors can explore the remains of luxurious Roman houses, public baths, and workshops, gaining insights into the daily lives of the town's ancient inhabitants. Interactive displays and multimedia presentations enhance the educational experience, making the museum a great destination for families and history buffs alike. The museum is open Tuesday to Sunday from 10:00 AM to 6:00 PM, with an admission fee of $8 per person. Guided tours are available for an additional fee, offering a more in-depth exploration of the site.

5. Pyramid of Vienne

Another notable landmark is the Pyramid of Vienne, a mysterious and unique monument that has intrigued historians and archaeologists for centuries. Standing at 15 meters high, this pyramid is believed to date back to the 2nd or 3rd century AD and is thought to have been part of a larger Roman circus or amphitheater. Its precise purpose remains a subject of debate, adding an element of intrigue to your visit.

The pyramid is located in a small park near the banks of the Rhone River, providing a peaceful setting to contemplate its enigmatic history. Informational plaques around the site offer various theories about its origin and function, allowing visitors to ponder its mysteries. The Pyramid of Vienne is accessible year-round, with no admission fee, making it a fascinating and budget-friendly addition to your historical tour.

6. Medieval and Renaissance Influences

While Vienne is renowned for its Roman heritage, it also boasts significant medieval and Renaissance landmarks that enrich its historical tapestry. The Cathedral of Saint Maurice, for instance, is a stunning example of Gothic architecture, with its construction spanning from the 12th to the 16th century. Its intricate façade and beautiful stained glass windows are a testament to the town's medieval artistic achievements.

Another noteworthy site is the Church of Saint Peter, one of the oldest surviving churches in France. Originally built in the 5th century and later modified in the Romanesque style, this church houses an impressive collection of religious art and artifacts. The church is open to visitors, with a small donation suggested for entry, supporting its preservation.

7. Roman Roads and Bridges

Exploring Vienne's ancient Roman roads and bridges offers a tangible connection to the town's historical infrastructure. The Pont Romain, a stone bridge that once facilitated trade and travel across the Rhone River, still stands as a testament to Roman engineering. Walking across this ancient bridge allows you to tread in the footsteps of merchants and travelers from centuries past.

Additionally, remnants of the Roman road network, including the Via Agrippa, can be traced throughout Vienne. These roads played a crucial role in the expansion and administration of the Roman Empire, linking Vienne to other major cities in Gaul. Exploring these ancient routes offers a unique perspective on the town's strategic importance in the Roman world.

8. Modern-Day Discoveries

While much of Vienne's ancient history is well-documented, ongoing archaeological excavations continue to uncover new insights and artifacts. These discoveries are often displayed in temporary exhibitions at the Gallo-Roman Museum, allowing visitors to witness the latest findings and understand their significance in the broader context of Roman history.

For those interested in the process of archaeology, the museum occasionally offers behind-the-scenes tours and workshops, providing a hands-on experience in uncovering the past. These activities are ideal for families and educational groups, fostering a deeper appreciation for the meticulous work involved in preserving history.

Getting to Vienne

Vienne is conveniently located within easy reach of major cities in the Rhone Valley, making it an accessible destination for travelers. The town is approximately 30 kilometers south of Lyon, France's third-largest city, and can be reached by train, car, or boat.

- By Train: Vienne is well-connected by the French rail network, with regular services from Lyon and other major cities. The journey from Lyon to Vienne takes around 20 minutes by train, making it a convenient day trip or an easy addition to your Rhone River cruise itinerary.
- By Car: If you prefer to drive, Vienne is accessible via the A7 motorway, which runs along the Rhone River. Ample parking is available in the town center, allowing you to explore its landmarks on foot.
- By Boat: Many Rhone River cruises include a stop in Vienne, providing a seamless and scenic way to visit the town. Disembark from your cruise ship and step directly into the heart of Vienne's historical treasures.

3.2.2 Cultural Immersion: Museums, Galleries, and Theaters

1. Musee des Beaux-Arts et d'Archeologie

The Musee des Beaux-Arts et d'Archeologie is a cornerstone of Vienne's cultural scene. Housed in a former Benedictine convent, this museum offers a diverse collection that spans various periods and styles, making it a must-visit for art enthusiasts and history buffs alike.

Collections and Exhibits

The museum's collection includes paintings, sculptures, and decorative arts from the Middle Ages to the 20th century. Highlights include works by regional artists, as well as pieces that illustrate the evolution of artistic movements over the centuries. The archaeology section features artifacts from Vienne's Roman past, including mosaics, pottery, and everyday objects that provide insight into ancient life.

Practical Information

- Address: Place de Miremont, 38200 Vienne, France
- Opening Hours: Tuesday to Sunday, 10:00 AM - 5:00 PM
- Admission Fee: $5 per person

Tips for Your Visit

To get the most out of your visit, consider joining a guided tour, which can provide deeper context and fascinating stories behind the exhibits. If you're visiting with children, check the museum's schedule for family-friendly activities and workshops designed to engage young minds.

2. Galerie Contemporaine

For a taste of contemporary art, head to Galerie Contemporaine. This vibrant gallery showcases the works of both emerging and established artists, providing a platform for creative expression and cultural dialogue.

Exhibitions and Programs

Galerie Contemporaine hosts a rotating schedule of exhibitions, ensuring there's always something new to see. The gallery often features solo shows, group exhibitions, and themed displays that highlight different aspects of contemporary art. Additionally, the gallery organizes workshops, artist talks, and community events, fostering a dynamic and inclusive cultural environment.

Practical Information

- Address: Rue des Arts, 38200 Vienne, France
- Opening Hours: Opening hours vary; check the gallery's website for details
- Admission Fee: Free admission

Tips for Your Visit

Keep an eye on the gallery's event calendar to coincide your visit with an opening reception or an artist talk. These events offer a unique opportunity to meet the artists and gain insight into their creative processes. Don't hesitate to engage with the gallery staff, who are often passionate about the exhibits and can provide valuable information and recommendations.

3. Theatre Antique de Vienne

The Theatre Antique de Vienne is a stunning example of Roman architecture and a cultural hub that hosts a variety of performances throughout the year. This ancient theater, with its impressive capacity and historical significance, is a highlight of any visit to Vienne.

Historical Significance

Built in the early 1st century AD, the Theatre Antique de Vienne could originally accommodate up to 13,000 spectators. It was used for various forms of entertainment, including plays, musical performances, and gladiatorial games. Today, it remains a central venue for cultural events, including the famous Jazz à Vienne festival.

Performances and Events

The theater's calendar is packed with a diverse range of performances, from classical music concerts to contemporary theater productions. The annual Jazz à Vienne festival is a particular highlight, attracting world-renowned artists and jazz enthusiasts from around the globe. Check the theater's schedule to see what performances coincide with your visit.

Practical Information

- Address: Montée Saint-Marcel, 38200 Vienne, France
- Opening Hours: Vary depending on scheduled events
- Admission Fee: Ticket prices vary depending on the event

Tips for Your Visit

Arrive early to secure a good seat and take in the theater's magnificent architecture before the performance begins. If you're visiting during the Jazz à Vienne festival, book your tickets in advance, as events often sell out quickly. Bring a cushion or blanket for added comfort during the performance, as the ancient stone seating can be quite hard.

4. The Modern Cultural Center

Vienne's commitment to cultural enrichment extends to its modern cultural center, which hosts a variety of events, exhibitions, and workshops throughout the year. This center serves as a vibrant community hub, bringing together locals and visitors to celebrate the arts.

Events and Exhibitions

The cultural center's program includes art exhibitions, film screenings, theatrical performances, and music concerts. The center also offers educational workshops and lectures, providing opportunities for cultural exchange and learning. Whether you're interested in visual arts, performing arts, or literary events, there's something for everyone.

Practical Information

- Address: Avenue du Général Leclerc, 38200 Vienne, France
- Opening Hours: Vary depending on scheduled events
- Admission Fee: Prices vary depending on the event

Tips for Your Visit

Check the cultural center's website for the latest program schedule and event details. If you're interested in a specific workshop or lecture, consider registering in advance to secure your spot. The center's cafe is a great place to relax and enjoy a coffee or light meal before or after your visit.

Street Art and Public Art Installations

Vienne's cultural immersion isn't confined to its museums and galleries. The town itself is a canvas, adorned with vibrant street art and public art installations that add color and creativity to its streets.

Exploring Vienne's Street Art

Take a leisurely stroll through Vienne's neighborhoods to discover murals, graffiti, and sculptures that reflect the town's artistic spirit. Local artists and visiting creatives have left their mark on Vienne's urban landscape, creating a dynamic and ever-evolving gallery of public art.

Notable Art Installations

Keep an eye out for notable installations such as the "Mosaic Wall," a collaborative project that features contributions from local artists and community members. Another highlight is the "River Sculpture," an abstract piece that pays homage to the Rhone River and its significance to the town.

Tips for Your Visit

Join a guided walking tour focused on Vienne's street art to gain deeper insights into the stories and artists behind the works. These tours often provide context and background that enhance your appreciation of the art. Alternatively, pick up a map from the local tourist office that highlights key locations of street art and public installations.

Local Music and Dance Performances

Vienne's cultural scene also includes a vibrant array of local music and dance performances. From traditional folk music to contemporary dance, there's a wealth of live entertainment to enjoy.

Live Music Venues

Several venues in Vienne regularly host live music performances, showcasing a range of genres from jazz and blues to classical and contemporary. The "Jazz Club" on Rue des Musiciens is a popular spot for intimate performances, while larger venues like the "Vienne Concert Hall" attract bigger acts and audiences.

Dance Performances

For dance enthusiasts, the "Ballet de Vienne" offers captivating performances that blend classical and modern styles. The dance troupe frequently performs at the "Cultural Center," where you can enjoy an evening of mesmerizing choreography and artistry.

Practical Information

1. Jazz Club: Rue des Musiciens, 38200 Vienne, France

- Opening Hours: Thursday to Saturday, 8:00 PM - 12:00 AM
- Admission Fee: $10 per person

2. Vienne Concert Hall: Place de la Musique, 38200 Vienne, France

- Opening Hours: Vary depending on scheduled events
- Admission Fee: Ticket prices vary depending on the event

3. Cultural Center: Avenue du Général Leclerc, 38200 Vienne, France

- Opening Hours: Vary depending on scheduled events
- Admission Fee: Prices vary depending on the event

Tips for Your Visit

Check the schedules of these venues to find performances that align with your interests. Many venues offer discounted tickets for students and seniors, so inquire about any available concessions. Arrive early to secure the best seats and enjoy pre-show drinks or snacks at the venue's bar or cafe.

3.2.3 Tasting the Terroir: Wine Tastings in the Rhone Valley

Embarking on a wine-tasting journey through the Rhone Valley is a sensory delight, offering an opportunity to savor the rich flavors and aromas that define these wines. Here, we'll explore some of the most esteemed wineries and vineyards, providing practical tips to enhance your tasting experience.

1. Domaine Georges Vernay: An Icon of Condrieu and Côte-Rôtie

Location and Overview

Domaine Georges Vernay is situated in Condrieu, a small appellation in the Northern Rhone renowned for its exceptional Viognier wines. Founded by Georges Vernay in the 1950s, the estate has played a pivotal role in reviving and promoting the Viognier grape variety. Today, it is managed by his daughter, Christine Vernay, who continues to produce world-class wines.

Wine Tasting Experience

A visit to Domaine Georges Vernay offers a comprehensive exploration of their esteemed wines. The estate specializes in Condrieu and Côte-Rôtie, with the former showcasing the aromatic richness of Viognier and the latter the depth and complexity of Syrah. During a guided tour, you'll learn about the vineyard's history, terroir, and winemaking techniques, culminating in a tasting session of their finest vintages.

Tips for Visiting

- Booking: Tastings are by appointment only, so it's advisable to book in advance through their website or contact them directly.
- Cost: A guided tour and tasting typically cost around $20 per person.
- Duration: Allocate at least 1.5 to 2 hours for the visit to fully appreciate the experience.
- Address: 1 Route Nationale 86, 69420 Condrieu, France

2. Maison M. Chapoutier: Tradition Meets Innovation

Location and Overview

Maison M. Chapoutier, located in Tain-l'Hermitage, is one of the most respected wineries in the Rhone Valley. Established in 1808, the estate is known for its commitment to biodynamic viticulture and its impressive portfolio of wines from both the Northern and Southern Rhone.

Wine Tasting Experience

At M. Chapoutier, visitors can choose from various tasting experiences, ranging from introductory tastings to more in-depth sessions that include vineyard tours. The winery's tasting room is modern and welcoming, providing a perfect setting to explore their wide range of wines, including Hermitage, Crozes-Hermitage, and Châteauneuf-du-Pape. Knowledgeable sommeliers guide you through the tasting, offering insights into the characteristics and production methods of each wine.

Tips for Visiting

- Booking: Advanced booking is recommended, especially for the more detailed tasting experiences.
- Cost: Tasting experiences start at approximately $15 per person, with more comprehensive tours priced higher.
- Duration: Plan for a visit of at least 2 hours to enjoy the full range of offerings.
- Address: 18 Avenue Dr. Paul Durand, 26600 Tain-l'Hermitage, France

3. Les Vins de Vienne: A Boutique Wine Experience

Location and Overview

Les Vins de Vienne is a boutique winery located in the heart of Vienne's old town. Founded by three friends, François Villard, Yves Cuilleron, and Pierre Gaillard, the winery produces a limited range of high-quality wines from select vineyard parcels in the Northern Rhone.

Wine Tasting Experience

The tasting room at Les Vins de Vienne exudes rustic charm, providing an intimate setting to sample their distinctive wines. The knowledgeable staff offers personalized tastings, allowing you to explore their elegant Syrahs, aromatic Viogniers, and other varietals. The emphasis here is on quality and authenticity, making it a must-visit for wine enthusiasts.

Tips for Visiting

- Booking: While walk-ins are welcome, it's best to call ahead to ensure availability.
- Cost: Tasting fees vary, typically starting at $10 per person.
- Duration: A tasting session usually lasts about 1 hour.
- Address: 24 Rue Marchande, 38200 Vienne, France

Tasting Tips and Etiquette

1. Preparing for Your Visit

- Stay Hydrated: Drink plenty of water to stay hydrated and to cleanse your palate between tastings.
- Eat Lightly: Have a light meal before your tasting to avoid drinking on an empty stomach, but avoid strong flavors that might affect your palate.
- Dress Comfortably: Wear comfortable shoes for walking through vineyards and layers to adjust to varying temperatures.

2. During the Tasting

- Engage with the Host: Don't hesitate to ask questions about the wines, the vineyard, and the winemaking process. Engaging with the host enhances your understanding and appreciation of the wines.
- Use All Your Senses: Observe the wine's color, swirl it in the glass to release aromas, and take small sips to fully experience the flavors and textures.
- Spit If Necessary: It's perfectly acceptable to spit the wine into the provided spittoon, especially if you're visiting multiple wineries.

3. Purchasing Wine

- Shipping Options: Many wineries offer shipping services, allowing you to send your favorite bottles home without the hassle of carrying them.
- Tasting Credits: Some wineries credit the tasting fee toward the purchase of wine, so be sure to inquire about this policy.

3.2.4 Culinary Delights: Sampling Vienne's Famous Cuisine

Vienne, with its historical roots and vibrant culture, provides a diverse culinary landscape that caters to all tastes. From Michelin-starred dining experiences to cozy bistros and delightful sweet treats, Vienne's culinary scene is a feast for the senses.

1. Michelin-Starred Excellence: Restaurant La Pyramide

Start your gastronomic adventure at Restaurant La Pyramide, a beacon of culinary excellence in Vienne. This renowned restaurant, helmed by Chef Patrick Henriroux, boasts two Michelin stars and a reputation for pushing the boundaries of French cuisine. The restaurant is located at 14 Boulevard Fernand Point, 38200 Vienne, France.

Chef Henriroux's menus are a symphony of flavors, with each dish meticulously crafted to showcase the finest seasonal ingredients. A typical dining experience at La Pyramide might include dishes such as foie gras with rhubarb and black sesame, or lobster with a hint of citrus and coriander. The prix-fixe menus, starting at approximately $80 per person, offer a journey through a series of artfully presented courses that highlight both traditional and innovative culinary techniques.

Opening Hours:

- Tuesday to Saturday: 12:00 PM - 1:30 PM for lunch, 7:30 PM - 9:00 PM for dinner
- Closed on Sundays and Mondays

2. Casual Dining with a Twist: Le Bistrot de la Galoche

For a more casual yet equally satisfying dining experience, Le Bistrot de la Galoche offers a warm and welcoming atmosphere. This charming bistro, located at 9 Rue de la Table Ronde, 38200 Vienne, France, is known for its hearty French fare infused with contemporary twists. The menu features classic dishes such as coq au vin, duck confit, and steak frites, all prepared with a focus on local ingredients and traditional methods.

One of the standout dishes is the boeuf bourguignon, a rich and flavorful beef stew simmered in red wine, which embodies the essence of French comfort food. The main courses range from $15 to $30 per person, making it an affordable option for travelers looking to enjoy an authentic meal without breaking the bank.

Opening Hours:

Daily: 12:00 PM - 2:30 PM for lunch, 7:00 PM - 10:00 PM for dinner

3. Sweet Indulgence: Chocolaterie Voisin

No visit to Vienne would be complete without indulging in the city's renowned pralines at Chocolaterie Voisin. This historic chocolatier, located at 13 Rue Boson, 38200 Vienne, France, has been a local institution since 1897. Voisin is celebrated for its exquisite chocolates, crafted using traditional recipes and the finest ingredients.

Step into the shop and be greeted by the intoxicating aroma of cocoa. Sample their famous pralines, which come in a variety of flavors, including hazelnut, almond, and pistachio, all encased in velvety chocolate. A box of assorted pralines starts at $10, making it an ideal souvenir or gift for loved ones back home.

Opening Hours:

- Monday to Saturday: 9:00 AM - 7:00 PM
- Closed on Sundays

For more information, visit their website or call +33 4 74 85 10 44. The shop's elegant displays and artisanal approach to chocolate-making provide a delightful treat for both the eyes and the taste buds.

4. Local Flavor: Les Halles de Vienne

For an immersive experience in Vienne's culinary culture, head to Les Halles de Vienne, the city's bustling covered market. Located at 14 Place Saint-Maurice, 38200 Vienne, France, this vibrant market is a haven for food lovers, offering a wide array of fresh produce, artisanal cheeses, and gourmet delights.

Wander through the market and sample local specialties such as saucisson (dry-cured sausage), various types of cheese like Saint-Marcellin and Reblochon, and freshly baked bread. Engage with the vendors, who are often eager to share the stories behind their products and offer tasting samples. This market experience not only provides a taste of local flavors but also a glimpse into the daily life of Vienne's residents.

Opening Hours:

- Tuesday to Sunday: 7:00 AM - 1:00 PM
- Closed on Mondays

Bring some cash, as some vendors may not accept credit cards. This market is an ideal spot to pick up ingredients for a picnic by the Rhone River or to find unique food items to bring back home.

Local Specialties: Must-Try Dishes

While exploring Vienne's culinary scene, be sure to try some of the local specialties that define the region's gastronomy. Here are a few must-try dishes:

- Gratin Dauphinois: A creamy potato gratin made with layers of thinly sliced potatoes, cream, and cheese, baked to golden perfection.
- Quenelles de Brochet: Light and fluffy dumplings made from pike fish, served with a rich crayfish or Nantua sauce.
- Tablier de Sapeur: A traditional Lyonnaise dish consisting of breaded and fried tripe, often served with a tangy sauce.

These dishes can be found at many restaurants throughout Vienne, offering a taste of the region's culinary heritage.

3.2.5 Shopping in Vienne: Markets and Boutiques

1. Les Halles de Vienne: A Culinary Paradise

Start your shopping adventure at Les Halles de Vienne, the town's bustling covered market. Located at 15 Rue des Carmes, this market is a haven for food enthusiasts and those looking to experience the local culture through its cuisine. Open from Tuesday to Sunday, from 7:00 AM to 1:00 PM, Les Halles is a sensory delight.

Here, you'll find an array of fresh produce, from vibrant vegetables to juicy fruits, sourced from local farms. Artisanal cheeses are another highlight; don't miss the chance to sample some of the region's finest varieties, such as Saint-Marcellin and Picodon. These cheeses are perfect for pairing with a fresh baguette for a picnic by the river.

For those with a sweet tooth, the market offers a selection of pastries and confections. Indulge in locally made macarons, nougat, and other sweet treats. Many stalls also sell gourmet products like olive oils, tapenades, and preserves, ideal for taking a piece of Vienne's culinary heritage home with you.

Tips for Visiting Les Halles de Vienne:

- Arrive early to enjoy the freshest selections and avoid the crowds.
- Bring a reusable shopping bag or basket, as vendors often do not provide bags.
- Engage with the vendors; many are happy to share samples and provide cooking tips.

2. Rue Marchande: The Heart of Vienne's Shopping District

Rue Marchande, Vienne's main shopping street, is a picturesque thoroughfare lined with charming boutiques and cafes. As you stroll along this historic street, you'll discover a variety of shops offering everything from fashion and accessories to home décor and souvenirs.

Start your exploration at Atelier du Souvenir (45 Rue Marchande), a boutique specializing in handcrafted gifts and souvenirs. Here, you'll find beautifully made items such as pottery, textiles, and jewelry, each reflecting the region's artisanal traditions. Whether you're looking for a unique piece of jewelry or a decorative item for your home, Atelier du Souvenir has something to offer.

Next, visit La Boutique des Artisans (38 Rue Marchande), where local artists and craftsmen showcase their creations. From hand-painted ceramics to intricately woven scarves, the shop's offerings are a testament to the skill and creativity of Vienne's artisans. This boutique is perfect for finding one-of-a-kind items that make excellent gifts or personal keepsakes.

For fashion enthusiasts, Mode et Passion (25 Rue Marchande) is a must-visit. This boutique features a curated selection of clothing and accessories from both local designers and well-known brands. Whether you're searching for a chic outfit or a stylish accessory, Mode et Passion offers a variety of options to suit your taste.

Tips for Shopping on Rue Marchande:

- Take your time to explore each boutique; many are small and packed with unique items.
- Enjoy a break at one of the street's charming cafes, where you can savor a coffee or pastry while people-watching.
- Keep an eye out for seasonal sales and promotions, especially during the summer and holiday seasons.

3. Place du Palais Weekly Market: A Community Gathering

Every Saturday morning, Place du Palais transforms into a bustling market where local farmers, artisans, and vendors come together to sell their goods. This weekly market, running from 8:00 AM to 1:00 PM, is a beloved tradition in

Vienne and a fantastic opportunity to experience the town's vibrant community spirit.

The market offers a wide range of fresh produce, including seasonal fruits and vegetables, flowers, and herbs. It's the perfect place to pick up ingredients for a picnic or to simply enjoy the sight and scent of fresh, locally grown produce.

Artisan stalls at Place du Palais showcase handcrafted items such as soaps, candles, and textiles. These make great gifts and souvenirs, offering a tangible connection to Vienne's rich artisanal heritage. You'll also find vendors selling prepared foods, from freshly baked bread to gourmet cheeses and charcuterie, ideal for assembling a delicious meal on the go.

Tips for Visiting Place du Palais Weekly Market:

- Arrive early for the best selection of fresh produce and artisanal goods.
- Bring cash, as some vendors may not accept credit cards.
- Take time to chat with the vendors; they often provide insights into their products and can recommend the best buys.

4. Specialty Shops and Boutiques: Unique Finds

Vienne's shopping scene is not limited to its main streets and markets. The town is dotted with specialty shops and boutiques, each offering unique products that reflect the region's culture and heritage.

Chocolaterie Voisin (10 Rue des Clercs) is a must-visit for chocolate lovers. Established in 1897, this renowned chocolatier offers an exquisite selection of chocolates and pralines, handcrafted using traditional recipes. Treat yourself to their famous pralines or pick up a beautifully packaged box to take home. The shop's elegant interior and the delightful aroma of chocolate make for an unforgettable shopping experience.

For wine enthusiasts, Cave de Vienne (8 Rue Joseph Brenier) is an excellent stop. This well-stocked wine shop offers a curated selection of local and regional wines, including the prestigious Côtes du Rhône and Châteauneuf-du-Pape. The knowledgeable staff can guide you through the selection, offering tasting notes and pairing suggestions to help you choose the perfect bottle.

L'Atelier de la Soie (12 Rue Teste du Bailler) is a boutique dedicated to the art of silk. Vienne has a long history of silk production, and this shop showcases beautiful silk scarves, ties, and fabrics, all crafted using traditional techniques. The luxurious textures and vibrant colors make these items both stylish and meaningful souvenirs.

Tips for Exploring Specialty Shops:

- Don't hesitate to ask shop owners about the history and production process of their goods; they are often passionate and knowledgeable.
- Look for locally made products to ensure you're bringing home an authentic piece of Vienne.
- Be mindful of shop opening hours, as some specialty shops may close for a lunch break or have limited hours on certain days.

Practical Information and Shopping Tips

When shopping in Vienne, a few practical tips can enhance your experience and help you make the most of your visit.

1. Currency and Payments:

- Most shops and markets accept Euros (€). While many places accept credit cards, it's a good idea to carry some cash, especially for market purchases and smaller boutiques.
- ATMs are available throughout the town, but be mindful of any fees your bank may charge for international withdrawals.

2. Tax-Free Shopping:

Visitors from outside the European Union can take advantage of tax-free shopping on purchases over a certain amount. Look for shops displaying the "Tax-Free Shopping" logo and ask the retailer for a tax refund form.

3. Shipping and Delivery:

If you're purchasing large or fragile items, ask the retailer about shipping options. Many shops offer international shipping services, allowing you to send your purchases directly home.

4. Respect Local Customs:

- Politeness goes a long way in Vienne. Always greet shopkeepers with a friendly "Bonjour" upon entering and a "Merci" when leaving.
- Bargaining is not common in France, so it's best to respect the listed prices.

3.3 Tournon-sur-Rhône and Tain-l'Hermitage: Wine Country Escapes

Tucked away amidst the rolling hills and vineyards of the Rhone Valley, Tournon-sur-Rhône and Tain-l'Hermitage offer a serene escape into the heart of French wine country.

As your river cruise gently glides into these charming ports of call, prepare to be enchanted by the beauty of the surrounding landscapes and the richness of the local wine culture.

3.3.1 Cruising Through the Picturesque Rhone Valley

As your cruise ship docks in Tournon-sur-Rhône or Tain-l'Hermitage, take the opportunity to embark on a leisurely stroll along the riverbanks. Breathe in the crisp, fresh air and admire the breathtaking views of lush vineyards stretching as far as the eye can see. Capture the moment with stunning photographs of the idyllic scenery and quaint riverside villages.

The Scenic Splendor of the Rhone Valley

The Rhone Valley is renowned for its stunning natural beauty. As your cruise ship sails through this enchanting region, you'll be treated to panoramic views of rolling hills covered in vineyards, lush green pastures, and the occasional glimpse of snow-capped peaks in the distance. The valley is a tapestry of colors and textures, with each turn of the river revealing new and breathtaking vistas.

Early mornings and late afternoons are particularly magical times to take in the scenery. The soft, golden light bathes the landscape in a warm glow, creating picture-perfect moments that are sure to be a highlight of your trip. Don't forget your camera, as there will be plenty of opportunities to capture the beauty of the Rhone Valley.

Exploring the Vineyards

One of the most iconic features of the Rhone Valley is its vineyards. This region is home to some of France's most prestigious wine appellations, including Côtes du Rhône, Châteauneuf-du-Pape, and Hermitage. As your cruise ship meanders through the valley, you'll see row upon row of meticulously tended grapevines stretching out across the hillsides.

To truly appreciate the region's viticulture, consider joining a guided vineyard tour. These excursions offer a unique opportunity to learn about the winemaking process, from the cultivation of the grapes to the aging of the wine. Knowledgeable guides will share insights into the history and traditions of Rhone Valley winemaking, as well as the characteristics that make these wines so exceptional.

Average Cost: Vineyard tours typically range from $50 to $100 per person, depending on the length of the tour and the number of tastings included.

Tip: Wear comfortable walking shoes and bring a hat and sunscreen, as you'll likely be spending a good amount of time outdoors. Also, consider scheduling your vineyard visit for the early morning or late afternoon to avoid the midday heat.

Tain-l'Hermitage: A Wine Lover's Paradise

Tain-l'Hermitage is one of the most celebrated wine-producing towns in the Rhone Valley. Located on the right bank of the Rhone River, this charming town is famous for its hillside vineyards that produce some of the finest Syrah and Marsanne wines in the world.

1. Domaine Chapoutier

One of the must-visit wineries in Tain-l'Hermitage is Domaine Chapoutier. This family-owned estate has been producing exceptional wines since 1808 and is known for its commitment to biodynamic viticulture. A visit to Domaine Chapoutier offers an in-depth look at the winemaking process and a chance to taste a variety of their acclaimed wines.

During your tour, you'll learn about the estate's biodynamic farming practices, which emphasize harmony with nature and sustainability. After the tour, enjoy a guided tasting of Domaine Chapoutier's wines, including their flagship Hermitage and Crozes-Hermitage wines. The tasting room is beautifully appointed, offering a relaxed and elegant setting to savor these exquisite wines.

Average Cost: A guided tour and tasting at Domaine Chapoutier typically costs around $30 to $50 per person.

2. Cave de Tain

Another notable winery in Tain-l'Hermitage is Cave de Tain. This cooperative winery was founded in 1933 and has grown to become one of the most respected producers in the region. Cave de Tain offers a range of wines, from everyday drinking options to premium selections.

A visit to Cave de Tain includes a guided tour of their modern winemaking facilities, where you'll see the state-of-the-art equipment used in the production process. After the tour, head to the tasting room to sample a selection of their wines. Knowledgeable staff will guide you through the tasting, providing information about each wine's characteristics and the terroir from which it comes.

Average Cost: A tour and tasting at Cave de Tain typically costs between $20 and $40 per person.

Tip: Make reservations in advance for both Domaine Chapoutier and Cave de Tain, especially during peak tourist season. This will ensure you secure a spot for your visit and avoid any disappointment.

Tournon-sur-Rhône: A Blend of History and Charm

Just across the river from Tain-l'Hermitage lies Tournon-sur-Rhône, a town steeped in history and charm. Tournon-sur-Rhône offers a variety of attractions that are perfect for a leisurely day of exploration.

1. Château de Tournon

One of the highlights of Tournon-sur-Rhône is the Château de Tournon, a medieval castle that dates back to the 10th century. Perched on a hill overlooking the Rhone River, the castle offers stunning views of the surrounding landscape. The château has been beautifully preserved and now houses a museum that showcases the history and heritage of the region.

As you explore the castle, you'll find a fascinating collection of artifacts, including medieval weaponry, period furniture, and historical documents. The château's towers and ramparts offer panoramic views of the Rhone Valley, making it a perfect spot for photography.

- Address: Rue de la Porte de l'Abbaye, 07300 Tournon-sur-Rhône, France
- Opening Hours: Tuesday-Sunday, 10:00 AM - 6:00 PM
- Admission: Adults $10, Children (under 12) $5

Tip: Arrive early in the day to avoid crowds and enjoy a more peaceful visit. The castle grounds are extensive, so allocate plenty of time to explore both the interior and the gardens.

2. Train de l'Ardèche

For a unique and scenic experience, take a ride on the Train de l'Ardèche. This historic steam train departs from Tournon-sur-Rhône and takes passengers on a picturesque journey through the Ardèche region. The train travels along a route that includes viaducts, tunnels, and beautiful countryside vistas.

As you sit back and relax in the vintage train cars, you'll be transported back in time to an era when steam locomotives ruled the rails. The journey offers stunning views of the Rhone Valley, with plenty of opportunities for photography along the way. The Train de l'Ardèche is a delightful way to experience the natural beauty of the region and learn about its railway heritage.

- Address: Gare de Tournon-Saint-Jean, 07300 Tournon-sur-Rhône, France
- Departure Times: Multiple departures daily, check website for schedule
- Ticket Prices: Adults $25, Children (ages 4-11) $15, Children (under 4) free

Tip: Purchase tickets in advance to secure your preferred departure time. The train can fill up quickly, especially during peak tourist season. Bring a camera to capture the scenic views along the route.

Culinary Delights of the Rhone Valley

No journey through the Rhone Valley would be complete without indulging in the region's culinary delights. The Rhone Valley is known for its rich gastronomic heritage, and there are plenty of opportunities to sample local specialties.

1. Local Markets

Visiting a local market is a fantastic way to experience the flavors of the Rhone Valley. Markets in towns like Tain-l'Hermitage and Tournon-sur-Rhône offer a wide variety of fresh produce, artisanal cheeses, cured meats, and baked goods. Stroll through the market stalls, engage with local vendors, and taste samples of regional specialties.

Tip: Markets are typically open in the mornings, so plan your visit accordingly. Bring some cash, as not all vendors accept credit cards.

2. Restaurants and Bistros

The Rhone Valley is home to numerous restaurants and bistros where you can enjoy delicious meals made with local ingredients. Whether you're looking for a casual lunch or a fine dining experience, you'll find plenty of options to suit your tastes.

In Tain-l'Hermitage, consider dining at Le Mangevins, a cozy bistro known for its creative cuisine and extensive wine list. The menu features seasonal dishes made with fresh, local ingredients, and the knowledgeable staff can recommend the perfect wine pairing for your meal.

- Address: 7 Place Auguste Faure, 26600 Tain-l'Hermitage, France
- Opening Hours: Tuesday-Saturday, 12:00 PM - 2:00 PM, 7:30 PM - 9:30 PM
- Average Cost: $30 to $50 per person, depending on the menu selection and wine pairings

In Tournon-sur-Rhône, visit Restaurant Le Quai for a memorable dining experience. Located on the banks of the Rhone River, this restaurant offers stunning views and a menu that showcases the best of Rhone Valley cuisine. Enjoy dishes such as duck confit, escargot, and local fish, all expertly prepared and beautifully presented.

- Address: 5 Quai Marc Seguin, 07300 Tournon-sur-Rhône, France
- Opening Hours: Tuesday-Sunday, 12:00 PM - 2:30 PM, 7:00 PM - 10:00 PM
- Average Cost: $40 to $60 per person, depending on the menu selection and wine pairings

3.3.2 *Wine Tasting in Tain-l'Hermitage: Domaine Chapoutier, Cave de Tain*

Among the most notable wineries are Domaine Chapoutier and Cave de Tain, both of which provide visitors with a deep dive into the rich history and exquisite flavors of the Rhone Valley wines.

1. Domaine Chapoutier: A Legacy of Excellence

History and Heritage

Domaine Chapoutier has been a cornerstone of the Rhone Valley winemaking tradition since 1808. With a commitment to biodynamic farming and a passion for producing wines that reflect the unique terroir of the region, Chapoutier has garnered international acclaim. The estate's philosophy is centered around respect for the environment, the vines, and the people who work the land, ensuring that every bottle produced is a true expression of its origin.

The Tasting Experience

A visit to Domaine Chapoutier is more than just a wine tasting; it is an educational journey into the art and science of winemaking. The tasting room, located at 18 Avenue Dr

Paul Durand, 26600 Tain-l'Hermitage, is open daily from 9:00 AM to 7:00 PM. Tastings are available by appointment, and it is advisable to book in advance, especially during peak tourist seasons.

Cost and Offerings

Domaine Chapoutier offers several tasting packages, ranging from basic tastings to more elaborate experiences that include vineyard tours and food pairings. Here are a few options:

- Classic Tasting: This option includes a guided tasting of five wines, highlighting different appellations and styles. Cost: $25 per person.
- Prestige Tasting: This includes a tasting of seven premium wines, including some of the estate's most acclaimed vintages. Cost: $50 per person.
- Vineyard Tour and Tasting: A guided tour of the vineyards followed by a comprehensive tasting of eight wines. Cost: $75 per person.

Tips for Getting the Most Out of Your Visit

- Book in Advance: Ensure you secure a spot by booking your tasting experience online or by phone.
- Learn the Terminology: Familiarize yourself with basic wine terminology to enhance your understanding and appreciation during the tasting.
- Ask Questions: The staff at Chapoutier are highly knowledgeable and passionate about their wines. Don't hesitate to ask questions about the winemaking process, the history of the estate, and the characteristics of the wines you are tasting.

2. Cave de Tain: Cooperative Excellence

Introduction to Cave de Tain

Founded in 1933, Cave de Tain is one of the most respected cooperative wineries in France. Located at 22 Route de Larnage, 26600 Tain-l'Hermitage, this cooperative brings together over 300 winegrowers who share a commitment to producing high-quality wines that showcase the unique terroir of the Rhone Valley.

The Tasting Experience

Visitors to Cave de Tain can expect a warm welcome and a comprehensive introduction to the cooperative's diverse range of wines. The tasting room is open Monday to Saturday from 9:30 AM to 6:30 PM and on Sundays from 10:00 AM to 6:00 PM. Tastings are conducted by knowledgeable staff who are eager to share their passion for winemaking.

Cost and Offerings

Cave de Tain offers a variety of tasting experiences designed to cater to different interests and levels of wine knowledge:

- Discovery Tasting: A guided tasting of five wines, showcasing different appellations and styles. Cost: $20 per person.
- Gourmet Tasting: Includes a tasting of seven wines paired with local cheeses and charcuterie. Cost: $35 per person.
- Premium Tasting: A tasting of ten top-tier wines, including prestigious Hermitage and Crozes-Hermitage wines. Cost: $50 per person.
- Private Tour and Tasting: A personalized tour of the winery followed by a tasting of twelve wines, including

limited edition and rare vintages. Cost: $100 per person.

Tips for Getting the Most Out of Your Visit

- Plan Your Visit: Check the opening hours and availability of tastings in advance, and consider visiting during weekdays to avoid the crowds.
- Explore the Vineyards: Take a walk through the vineyards surrounding the cooperative to fully appreciate the landscape that contributes to the unique characteristics of the wines.
- Take Notes: Bring a notebook to jot down your impressions of each wine, along with any interesting information shared by the staff.

3. Tain-l'Hermitage and Tournon-sur-Rhône: Beyond the Wineries

While the wine tastings at Domaine Chapoutier and Cave de Tain are undoubtedly the highlights of your visit, the towns of Tain-l'Hermitage and Tournon-sur-Rhône offer much more to explore.

a. Château de Tournon

Perched on a hill overlooking the Rhone River, Château de Tournon is a must-visit historical site. This medieval fortress, dating back to the 10th century, offers stunning views of the surrounding vineyards and river. The castle houses a museum with exhibits on the history of the region, the castle itself, and its former inhabitants.

- Address: Rue de la Porte de l'Abbaye, 07300 Tournon-sur-Rhône, France
- Opening Hours: Tuesday-Sunday, 10:00 AM - 6:00 PM

- Admission: Adults $10, Children (under 12) $5

b. Train de l'Ardèche

For a unique and scenic experience, hop aboard the Train de l'Ardèche, a historic steam train that travels through the picturesque landscapes of the Ardèche region. This journey offers breathtaking views of the Rhone Valley, including viaducts, tunnels, and rolling vineyards.

- Address: Gare de Tournon-Saint-Jean, 07300 Tournon-sur-Rhône, France
- Departure Times: Multiple departures daily, check website for schedule
- Ticket Prices: Adults $25, Children (ages 4-11) $15, Children (under 4) free

Local Cuisine and Dining

No visit to the Rhone Valley is complete without indulging in the local cuisine. Both Tain-l'Hermitage and Tournon-sur-Rhône boast a variety of dining options, from quaint bistros to gourmet restaurants.

1. Le Quai Restaurant

Situated along the riverfront, Le Quai offers a delightful dining experience with a menu featuring regional specialties and fresh, locally sourced ingredients. The outdoor terrace provides a perfect setting for enjoying a meal while taking in the scenic views of the Rhone River.

- Address: 6 Quai Farconnet, 07300 Tournon-sur-Rhône, France
- Opening Hours: Daily, 12:00 PM - 10:00 PM
- Average Cost: $40 per person

2. Restaurant Michel Chabran

For a more upscale dining experience, head to Restaurant Michel Chabran, a Michelin-starred establishment renowned for its exquisite cuisine and elegant ambiance. The menu features innovative dishes that blend traditional French flavors with modern culinary techniques.

- Address: 29 Avenue du 45ème Parallèle, 26600 Pont-de-l'Isère, France
- Opening Hours: Tuesday-Saturday, 12:00 PM - 2:00 PM and 7:00 PM - 9:30 PM
- Average Cost: $100 per person

Shopping and Souvenirs

Take some time to explore the local shops and markets in Tain-l'Hermitage and Tournon-sur-Rhône. You will find a variety of unique souvenirs, including local wines, gourmet foods, and handcrafted goods.

1. Maison Chapoutier Boutique

Located adjacent to the tasting room, the Maison Chapoutier Boutique offers an extensive selection of the estate's wines, along with gourmet products such as olive oils, vinegars, and chocolates. It is the perfect place to pick up a bottle of your favorite wine or a thoughtful gift for friends and family.

- Address: 18 Avenue Dr Paul Durand, 26600 Tain-l'Hermitage, France
- Opening Hours: Daily, 9:00 AM - 7:00 PM

2. Cave de Tain Shop

The Cave de Tain shop features a wide range of wines produced by the cooperative, as well as local delicacies and wine accessories. Be sure to check out their selection of limited edition and rare vintages, which make for excellent souvenirs or additions to your wine collection.

- Address: 22 Route de Larnage, 26600 Tain-l'Hermitage, France
- Opening Hours: Monday-Saturday, 9:30 AM - 6:30 PM; Sunday, 10:00 AM - 6:00 PM

3.3.3 Exploring Tournon-sur-Rhône: Château de Tournon, Train de l'Ardèche

1. Château de Tournon: A Medieval Marvel

Perched majestically atop a hill, the Château de Tournon dominates the skyline of Tournon-sur-Rhône. This imposing medieval fortress, with its rugged stone walls and towering turrets, offers a fascinating journey through time, providing visitors with a deep dive into the history and culture of the region.

A Brief History

The origins of Château de Tournon date back to the 10th century, though much of the current structure was built between the 14th and 16th centuries. Originally constructed as a defensive stronghold, it later became the residence of the Counts of Tournon. The castle's strategic location overlooking the Rhone River made it a crucial site for controlling trade and travel along this vital waterway.

Exploring the Castle

Upon entering the castle, visitors are greeted by a blend of Gothic and Renaissance architecture. The stone archways, grand halls, and intricate tapestries transport you back to a time of knights and nobility. One of the highlights is the Great Hall, where the grandeur of the medieval period is on full display. The hall's high ceilings, adorned with wooden beams, and the large stone fireplace evoke the ambiance of historic feasts and gatherings.

Exhibits and Collections

The Château de Tournon houses an impressive collection of artifacts and exhibits that chronicle the history of the region. Visitors can explore exhibits on medieval weaponry, showcasing swords, armor, and crossbows. The castle's chapel, with its beautiful stained-glass windows, offers a serene space for reflection.

One of the most captivating parts of the castle is the collection of Renaissance paintings and sculptures. These artworks provide a glimpse into the cultural and artistic achievements of the period. Don't miss the stunning views from the castle's terraces, which offer panoramic vistas of the Rhone River and the surrounding vineyards.

Practical Information

- Address: Rue de la Porte de l'Abbaye, 07300 Tournon-sur-Rhône, France
- Opening Hours: Tuesday-Sunday, 10:00 AM - 6:00 PM
- Admission: Adults $10, Children (under 12) $5

Tips for Visiting

To make the most of your visit to the Château de Tournon, plan to arrive early in the day. This not only helps you avoid the crowds but also allows you ample time to explore the castle at a leisurely pace. Comfortable walking shoes are recommended, as there are several steep and uneven pathways within the castle grounds.

For history enthusiasts, guided tours are available and provide deeper insights into the castle's storied past. Be sure to check the château's website or contact their visitor center for information on special events, such as medieval reenactments or seasonal exhibitions, which can enhance your experience.

2. Train de l'Ardèche: A Scenic Journey Through Time

After immersing yourself in the medieval splendor of the Château de Tournon, embark on a different kind of adventure with the Train de l'Ardèche. This historic steam train offers a nostalgic journey through the breathtaking landscapes of the Ardèche region, providing an unforgettable travel experience.

The Journey Begins

The Train de l'Ardèche departs from the Gare de Tournon-Saint-Jean, located in Tournon-sur-Rhône. As you step aboard the beautifully restored carriages, you'll feel as though you've traveled back in time to the golden age of steam railways. The train's vintage charm, complete with wooden seats and brass fittings, adds to the nostalgic ambiance.

Scenic Routes and Panoramic Views

The train winds its way through the scenic Ardèche countryside, passing through vineyards, forests, and charming villages. The route includes several viaducts and tunnels, offering dramatic views of the Rhone Valley and the Doux River. One of the highlights of the journey is crossing the Gorges du Doux, where the train navigates narrow passages and steep cliffs, providing breathtaking views of the river below.

Onboard Experience

During the journey, knowledgeable guides share fascinating stories and historical anecdotes about the region and the railway itself. The rhythmic chugging of the steam engine and the gentle sway of the carriages create a relaxing and immersive experience. The train's large windows provide unobstructed views, perfect for capturing stunning photographs of the passing landscapes.

Stops Along the Way

The Train de l'Ardèche makes several stops along its route, allowing passengers to disembark and explore the local area. One notable stop is at Colombier-le-Vieux, where you can visit a traditional Ardèche market and sample local delicacies. Another stop at Boucieu-le-Roi offers a chance to explore a charming village known for its historic architecture and peaceful ambiance.

Practical Information

- Address: Gare de Tournon-Saint-Jean, 07300 Tournon-sur-Rhône, France
- Departure Times: Multiple departures daily, check website for schedule
- Ticket Prices: Adults $25, Children (ages 4-11) $15, Children (under 4) free

Tips for Riding the Train

To ensure a memorable journey on the Train de l'Ardèche, it's advisable to book your tickets in advance, especially during peak tourist seasons. The train operates year-round, but the schedule may vary, so checking the official website for the latest information is recommended.

For the best views, try to secure a seat on the right side of the train when departing from Tournon-sur-Rhône, as this side often offers the most scenic vistas. If you're traveling with children, the train ride is a wonderful family-friendly activity, and the stops along the route provide opportunities for little ones to stretch their legs and explore.

Combining Both Experiences

For those seeking a comprehensive exploration of Tournon-sur-Rhône, combining a visit to the Château de Tournon with a ride on the Train de l'Ardèche offers a perfect blend of history, culture, and natural beauty.

a. Morning at the Château

Begin your day with a visit to the Château de Tournon. Arriving early will give you plenty of time to delve into the castle's exhibits and enjoy the panoramic views from its terraces. Take a leisurely stroll through the castle's grounds and imagine the lives of the medieval inhabitants who once called this fortress home.

b. Lunch in Town

After your castle visit, head down to the town of Tournon-sur-Rhône for a delightful lunch. The town boasts several charming cafes and restaurants where you can savor local cuisine. For a true taste of the region, try dishes featuring fresh, seasonal ingredients, such as river fish, wild mushrooms, and regional cheeses. Pair your meal with a glass of Côtes du Rhône wine for a complete culinary experience.

c. Afternoon on the Train

In the afternoon, make your way to the Gare de Tournon-Saint-Jean to board the Train de l'Ardèche. The train journey will provide a relaxing and scenic way to spend the rest of your day, as you traverse the stunning landscapes of the Ardèche region. Enjoy the commentary provided by the guides and take in the breathtaking views from the comfort of your vintage carriage.

d. Evening Relaxation

Upon your return to Tournon-sur-Rhône, unwind with a leisurely walk along the riverbanks. The town's riverside promenade is particularly enchanting in the early evening, with the golden light reflecting off the water and the silhouette of the Château de Tournon creating a picturesque backdrop. If you have time, stop by one of the local patisseries for a sweet treat before heading back to your cruise ship.

3.4 Arles: Van Gogh's Inspirational Haven

Nestled in the heart of Provence, Arles beckons travelers with its timeless beauty and artistic allure. As the city that captured Vincent Van Gogh's imagination and inspired some of his most iconic works, Arles continues to enchant visitors with its picturesque streets, ancient landmarks, and vibrant cultural scene.

3.4.1 Walking in Van Gogh's Footsteps: Sites Related to the Artist's Life

Arles, a charming city in the heart of Provence, holds a unique place in the annals of art history. It was here, between 1888 and 1889, that Vincent Van Gogh created some of his most celebrated works. His time in Arles was marked by prolific creativity, despite personal turmoil, and the city itself became an enduring muse. For art lovers and curious travelers alike, walking in Van Gogh's footsteps in Arles offers a deeply enriching experience. This guide highlights the must-visit sites related to the artist's life, providing insights and practical tips to make the most of your journey.

Espace Van Gogh

Your Van Gogh pilgrimage should begin at the Espace Van Gogh (Place Félix Rey, 13200 Arles, France), a site steeped in the artist's history. Originally the hospital where Van Gogh was admitted after his infamous ear-cutting incident, this historic building has been transformed into a cultural center. The courtyard, now filled with vibrant flowers and a serene fountain, is depicted in several of Van Gogh's paintings, offering a real-life glimpse into his artistic vision.

Inside, the Espace Van Gogh houses various exhibitions dedicated to his work and legacy. These exhibits provide a comprehensive overview of his time in Arles, complete with reproductions of his paintings, letters, and multimedia displays that narrate his life story. Admission fees range from $10 to $15, making it an affordable start to your artistic adventure.

Practical Tip: Allocate at least an hour to explore the Espace Van Gogh. The peaceful ambiance of the courtyard is perfect for contemplation, so take your time to absorb the surroundings that once inspired the artist.

The Van Gogh Walking Tour

To fully immerse yourself in Van Gogh's Arles, embark on the Van Gogh Walking Tour. This self-guided tour is well-marked with signposts featuring reproductions of Van

Gogh's paintings placed at the locations where he painted them. This unique approach allows you to see the city through the artist's eyes and understand his perspective.

Key Sites on the Tour:

- Café Terrace at Night: One of Van Gogh's most famous works, this painting captures the bustling evening atmosphere of a café in the Place du Forum. The café, now named Café Van Gogh (Place du Forum, 13200 Arles, France), retains its vibrant yellow facade, inviting visitors to sit and savor a drink where Van Gogh once found inspiration. A café gourmand here costs around $8 to $12, offering a delightful taste of local pastries alongside your coffee.

- The Yellow House: Located at the corner of Place Lamartine, the site of Van Gogh's residence is marked by a signpost displaying his painting of the house. While the original building was destroyed during World War II, standing at this location offers a poignant connection to Van Gogh's dream of establishing an artists' colony.

- The Public Garden: Van Gogh painted several scenes of Arles' public gardens, including the Garden of the Hospital in Arles. These gardens, now part of the Van Gogh Trail, are beautifully maintained and offer a tranquil spot for reflection.

- The Rhône River: Van Gogh's Starry Night Over the Rhône was inspired by the riverbanks near Place Lamartine. Walking along the Rhône, particularly at twilight, allows you to experience the same captivating light that inspired Van Gogh's brushstrokes.

- Practical Tip: The Van Gogh Walking Tour can be completed at your own pace, but a guided tour ($20-

$30 per person) can enhance the experience with additional historical context and anecdotes about Van Gogh's life in Arles.

Vincent Van Gogh Foundation

For a deeper dive into the artist's legacy, visit the Vincent Van Gogh Foundation (35 Rue du Docteur Fanton, 13200 Arles, France). This modern museum is dedicated to showcasing both Van Gogh's works and contemporary art influenced by his legacy. The foundation regularly hosts exhibitions that juxtapose Van Gogh's masterpieces with works by modern artists, creating a dialogue between the past and present.

The museum's collection includes a mix of original Van Gogh pieces and those from private collections and other museums. Multimedia displays and interactive installations provide a comprehensive understanding of his artistic journey. Admission ranges from $12 to $20, and the foundation is open daily from 10 AM to 6 PM, except on Mondays.

Practical Tip: Check the foundation's website for current exhibitions and special events. Visiting during an exhibition can provide additional insights into Van Gogh's impact on contemporary art.

Café Van Gogh

A visit to Arles would be incomplete without stopping by the iconic Café Van Gogh (Place du Forum, 13200 Arles, France). Immortalized in Van Gogh's painting Café Terrace at Night, this bustling café still exudes the charm and ambiance captured by the artist.

The café's bright yellow exterior stands out in the historic Place du Forum, making it a perfect spot for photos. Inside, the atmosphere is lively, with locals and tourists mingling over coffee and Provençal dishes. Prices are reasonable, with a café gourmand (a coffee served with a selection of mini desserts) costing around $8 to $12.

Practical Tip: Visit in the evening to experience the café as Van Gogh did, with the warm glow of street lamps and the vibrant energy of the square. It's an ideal spot for unwinding after a day of exploring.

The Alyscamps

Van Gogh's fascination with cemeteries led him to paint several scenes of the Alyscamps, an ancient Roman necropolis located just outside the city center (Avenue des Alyscamps, 13200 Arles, France). The site is characterized by its long avenue lined with sarcophagi, creating a hauntingly beautiful setting.

Van Gogh often visited the Alyscamps with fellow artist Paul Gauguin, and their collaborative works capture the serene yet eerie ambiance of the site. Today, the Alyscamps is open to visitors, with an entrance fee of $5 to $10. The site offers a peaceful escape from the city's hustle and provides a unique perspective on Van Gogh's artistic process.

Practical Tip: Visit the Alyscamps in the late afternoon when the light is softer, enhancing the site's mystical atmosphere. Allow at least an hour to explore and take in the serene surroundings.

Langlois Bridge

One of Van Gogh's favorite painting subjects in Arles was the Langlois Bridge, also known as the Pont de Langlois (Route de Fontvieille, 13200 Arles, France). This drawbridge, depicted in several of his works, symbolized the pastoral beauty of Provence. Though the original bridge was replaced, a replica now stands in its place, providing a picturesque spot reminiscent of Van Gogh's paintings.

The surrounding area offers lovely walking and cycling paths, making it an ideal location for a leisurely afternoon. You can pack a picnic and enjoy the serene landscape, much like Van Gogh did during his painting sessions.

Practical Tip: Rent a bicycle from a local shop for around $15-$20 per day and explore the scenic routes around the Langlois Bridge. The ride offers a blend of natural beauty and artistic heritage.

Fondation LUMA Arles

While not directly related to Van Gogh, the Fondation LUMA Arles (Parc des Ateliers, 45 Avenue Victor Hugo, 13200 Arles, France) is a contemporary art center that celebrates the creative spirit of the region. Opened in 2013, LUMA Arles hosts exhibitions, performances, and workshops, fostering a vibrant cultural scene.

The foundation's striking architecture, designed by Frank Gehry, is a work of art in itself. Admission fees vary depending on the exhibition, typically ranging from $10 to $20. The foundation is open daily from 10 AM to 7 PM, offering ample opportunities to explore its diverse programs.

Practical Tip: Check the foundation's calendar for special events and exhibitions. Visiting during a major exhibition can provide a dynamic counterpoint to your exploration of Van Gogh's historic sites.

Arles Market

For a taste of local life, visit the Arles Market (Boulevard des Lices, 13200 Arles, France), held every Wednesday and Saturday morning. This bustling market is one of the largest in Provence, offering a vibrant array of local produce, artisanal goods, and regional specialties.

While not directly tied to Van Gogh, the market's lively atmosphere and colorful stalls evoke the spirit of Provençal life that inspired many of his works. Take your time to wander through the market, sampling fresh cheeses, olives, and pastries. Prices are reasonable, with many vendors offering generous samples of their wares.

Practical Tip: Arrive early to experience the market at its peak and avoid the midday crowds. Bring cash, as many vendors may not accept credit cards.

Arles Amphitheater and Théâtre Antique

To round out your exploration, visit the Arles Amphitheater (Rue de la Calade, 13200 Arles, France) and the Théâtre Antique (Rue de la Calade, 13200 Arles, France). These ancient Roman sites offer a fascinating glimpse into the city's history and provide context for Van Gogh's fascination with Arles' architectural heritage.

The amphitheater, one of the best-preserved Roman arenas in the world, hosts various events, including bullfights and concerts. The nearby Théâtre Antique offers panoramic views of the city and serves as a venue for cultural performances. Admission fees for these sites range from $8 to $12.

Practical Tip: Visit the amphitheater and theater early in the day to avoid the heat and crowds. Consider attending a performance if your visit coincides with one of the scheduled events.

3.4.2 Roman Heritage: Arles' Amphitheater and Ancient Architecture

1. The Arles Amphitheater

The Arles Amphitheater, or Les Arènes d'Arles, is arguably the most iconic Roman structure in the city. Built in 90 AD, this impressive arena could originally seat up to 20,000 spectators. It was designed primarily for gladiatorial contests and public spectacles, much like the Colosseum in Rome.

- Location: Rue de la Calade, 13200 Arles, France

Opening Hours:

- April to September: 9:00 AM - 7:00 PM
- October to March: 10:00 AM - 5:00 PM

Admission Fees:

- Adults: $10
- Students and Seniors: $8
- Children (7-17): $5
- Free for children under 7

The amphitheater is a marvel of Roman engineering, with two tiers of 60 arches, and it remains remarkably well-preserved. Today, it continues to be a focal point for cultural activities, hosting events such as the Feria d'Arles, which includes traditional bullfighting, concerts, and theater performances. Walking through the stone corridors and sitting in the ancient stands, you can almost hear the roar of the crowds from centuries past.

Tip: Visit early in the morning or late in the afternoon to avoid the crowds and experience the amphitheater in a more serene atmosphere. Guided tours are available and highly recommended to gain deeper insights into the history and architecture of this ancient marvel.

2. The Roman Theater

Just a short walk from the amphitheater, you'll find the Roman Theater of Arles. Constructed in the late 1st century BC, this theater was one of the first examples of Roman entertainment architecture in France. It originally had a seating capacity of about 10,000 spectators and was used for theatrical performances, which were an integral part of Roman cultural life.

- Location: Rue de la Calade, 13200 Arles, France

Opening Hours:

- April to September: 9:00 AM - 7:00 PM
- October to March: 10:00 AM - 5:00 PM

Admission Fees:

- Adults: $8
- Students and Seniors: $6
- Children (7-17): $4
- Free for children under 7

While much of the theater has been lost to time, the stage, orchestra, and some of the tiered seating remain. The theater is still used today for summer performances and the annual Arles International Photography Festival. The juxtaposition of ancient ruins with contemporary performances creates a unique cultural experience.

Tip: Check the schedule of events before your visit. Attending a performance in this ancient venue adds an unforgettable dimension to your visit.

3. The Cryptoporticus

Hidden beneath the Place du Forum lies one of Arles' most fascinating Roman structures: the Cryptoporticus. This semi-subterranean structure was built in the 1st century BC and served as a foundation for the forum above, providing both support and storage space. The Cryptoporticus is a series of three long, parallel vaulted corridors, forming an underground gallery that offers a cool retreat on a hot day.

- Location: Place du Forum, 13200 Arles, France

Opening Hours:

- April to September: 10:00 AM - 6:00 PM
- October to March: 10:00 AM - 5:00 PM

Admission Fees:

- Adults: $5
- Students and Seniors: $4
- Children (7-17): $3
- Free for children under 7

Exploring the Cryptoporticus provides a unique perspective on Roman engineering and urban planning. The dimly lit, ancient corridors evoke a sense of mystery and adventure, making it a favorite among history enthusiasts and adventurous travelers alike.

Tip: Wear comfortable shoes as the ground can be uneven, and bring a light jacket as it can be cool underground.

4. The Alyscamps

Just outside the city center, the Alyscamps is an ancient Roman necropolis that has been a burial site since Roman times. The name Alyscamps comes from the Latin "Elisii

Campi," meaning Elysian Fields. The site was once a major Christian burial ground, and in the Middle Ages, it became one of the most famous necropolises in Western Europe, attracting visitors from far and wide.

- Location: Avenue des Alyscamps, 13200 Arles, France

Opening Hours:

- April to September: 9:00 AM - 7:00 PM
- October to March: 10:00 AM - 5:00 PM

Admission Fees:

- Adults: $8
- Students and Seniors: $6
- Children (7-17): $4
- Free for children under 7

As you walk along the ancient path lined with sarcophagi, you'll pass the remains of the Church of Saint-Honorat and the Church of Saint-Césaire-le-Vieux. The Alyscamps is a peaceful, evocative site, providing a quiet escape from the bustling city streets and a poignant reminder of the passage of time.

Tip: Visit in the late afternoon when the light is soft and golden, enhancing the mystical atmosphere of the site.

5. The Baths of Constantine

The Thermae of Constantine are the remains of a Roman bath complex dating back to the 4th century AD. These baths were an essential part of Roman social life, serving not only as a place for bathing but also for socializing and conducting business.

- Location: Rue du Grand Prieuré, 13200 Arles, France

Opening Hours:

- April to September: 9:00 AM - 7:00 PM
- October to March: 10:00 AM - 5:00 PM

Admission Fees:

- Adults: $6
- Students and Seniors: $4
- Children (7-17): $3
- Free for children under 7

The remains include the frigidarium (cold room), tepidarium (warm room), and caldarium (hot room). The vaulted ceilings and large windows of the frigidarium are particularly impressive, showcasing the architectural ingenuity of the Romans.

Tip: Combine your visit to the baths with a walk along the Rhone River, which offers beautiful views and a pleasant atmosphere.

6. The Roman Walls

Arles was once surrounded by imposing Roman walls, built to protect the city from invaders. While much of the original structure has been lost, several sections of these ancient fortifications still stand today, offering a glimpse into the city's defensive past.

Location: Various points around the city, including the Place de la République and the Rue du 4 Septembre

These walls, constructed in the 4th century AD, were part of a larger system of fortifications that included towers and gates. Walking along these ancient remnants, you can imagine the strategic importance of Arles in Roman times.

Tip: Take a guided tour to learn more about the history and significance of the walls and other Roman structures in the city.

7. The Church of St. Trophime

Although not strictly Roman, the Church of St. Trophime is a must-see for its exquisite Romanesque architecture and its roots in the ancient Roman period. The church, built in the 12th century, stands on the site of an earlier basilica dating back to the 5th century.

- Location: Place de la République, 13200 Arles, France

Opening Hours:

- Monday to Saturday: 9:00 AM - 12:00 PM, 2:00 PM - 5:00 PM
- Sunday: 2:00 PM - 5:00 PM

Admission Fees:

- Free entry

The church's stunning portal, adorned with detailed sculptures depicting scenes from the Last Judgment, is a masterpiece of Romanesque art. Inside, you'll find a serene atmosphere, beautiful chapels, and the relics of St. Trophime, the city's patron saint.

Tip: Visit during the quiet hours of the morning or late afternoon to appreciate the church's beauty without the crowds.

3.4.3 Provençal Charm: Exploring the Streets and Cafés
A Stroll Through Time: The Streets of Arles

Arles' streets are a living museum, echoing with stories from its Roman past to its artistic renaissance. Begin your exploration in the heart of the Old Town, where narrow lanes twist and turn, leading to hidden courtyards and picturesque squares.

The Place du Forum is a great starting point. Once the center of Roman life in Arles, today it's a bustling square filled with cafés and restaurants. Here, you'll find the famous Café la Nuit (Place du Forum, 13200 Arles, France), depicted in Van Gogh's painting "Café Terrace at Night." Sit under the same starry sky that inspired the artist and enjoy a Café Gourmand – a coffee served with a selection of mini desserts – for about $8-$12.

As you leave the Place du Forum, head towards the Rue de la Liberté. This street is lined with charming boutiques selling local crafts, Provençal fabrics, and artisanal soaps. Don't miss Le Panier d'Arles (1 Rue de la Liberté, 13200 Arles, France), a delightful shop where you can find authentic Provençal goods to take home.

Wandering further, you'll come across the Place de la République, dominated by the striking Saint-Trophime Church (Place de la République, 13200 Arles, France). This Romanesque masterpiece is known for its intricately carved portal and serene cloisters. Admission is free, but donations are welcome. The church is open daily from 9:00 AM to 7:00 PM, with shorter hours on Sundays.

Hidden Gems and Local Flavors

Arles is a city meant for leisurely exploration. Take your time to discover its hidden gems, such as the Cour de l'Archevêché, a tranquil courtyard where you can escape the hustle and bustle of the main streets. Nearby, you'll find Le

Comptoir des Porcelaines (8 Rue des Porcelets, 13200 Arles, France), a small shop offering exquisite porcelain pieces, perfect for a unique souvenir.

No visit to Arles is complete without experiencing its vibrant markets. The Arles Market (Boulevard des Lices, 13200 Arles, France) takes place every Wednesday and Saturday morning from 8:00 AM to 1:00 PM. It's one of the largest and most colorful markets in Provence, featuring a dazzling array of fresh produce, cheeses, olives, spices, and local delicacies. Stroll through the stalls, sample some tapenade or lavender honey, and immerse yourself in the lively atmosphere.

For lunch, head to Le Café Van Gogh (Place du Forum, 13200 Arles, France), where you can enjoy traditional Provençal dishes under the shade of ancient plane trees. Try the Daube Provençale – a hearty beef stew slow-cooked in red wine – for about $20-$30. The café also offers a variety of local wines, providing the perfect opportunity to sample some of the region's best vintages.

Café Culture and Provençal Cuisine

The café culture in Arles is an integral part of its charm. Cafés here are more than just places to grab a quick coffee; they are social hubs where locals and visitors alike gather to relax, converse, and watch the world go by.

One such spot is Le Café des Alyscamps (18 Rue des Porcelets, 13200 Arles, France), situated near the ancient Alyscamps necropolis. This quaint café offers a peaceful retreat with its shaded terrace and delicious homemade pastries. A typical coffee and pastry combo will set you back around $8-$10.

For a truly local experience, visit La Gueule du Loup (39 Rue des Arènes, 13200 Arles, France), a bistro renowned for its creative Provençal cuisine. The menu changes with the seasons, showcasing the freshest local ingredients. Expect to pay around $40-$60 for a three-course meal.

Arles is also home to several wine bars where you can sample the region's finest wines. Le Petit Arles (14 Rue de la Liberté, 13200 Arles, France) offers an extensive selection of wines by the glass, along with charcuterie and cheese boards. Enjoy a leisurely evening here, savoring local vintages in a relaxed setting.

Seasonal Festivals and Events

Arles comes alive with festivals and events throughout the year, offering visitors a chance to experience the city's vibrant culture. One of the most famous is the Feria d'Arles, held twice a year in April and September. This traditional festival features bullfights, parades, and lively street parties. If your visit coincides with the Feria, be sure to join in the festivities and experience the city's exuberant spirit.

Another highlight is the Rencontres d'Arles, an international photography festival held from July to September. The festival transforms the city into an open-air gallery, with exhibitions and installations spread across various venues. It's a must-see for photography enthusiasts and art lovers alike.

During the holiday season, the Christmas Market (Place de la République, 13200 Arles, France) is a delightful place to visit. From late November to early January, the square is filled with stalls selling festive decorations, handmade gifts, and seasonal treats. Enjoy a cup of mulled wine as you browse the market and soak in the holiday cheer.

Tips for Getting the Most Out of Your Visit

To make the most of your time in Arles, consider these practical tips:

- Plan Ahead: Arles is best explored on foot, so wear comfortable shoes and plan your itinerary to include both must-see attractions and hidden gems.
- Embrace Local Customs: The pace of life in Provence is relaxed, so take your time to enjoy leisurely meals, strolls, and conversations with locals.
- Visit Early or Late: To avoid the crowds, visit popular sites like the Arles Amphitheater and Place du Forum early in the morning or late in the afternoon.
- Learn Some French Phrases: While many locals speak English, learning a few basic French phrases can enhance your experience and show respect for the local culture.
- Try Local Specialties: Don't miss out on Provençal dishes like Bouillabaisse (fish stew), Ratatouille (vegetable stew), and Tarte Tropézienne (a cream-filled brioche).

Practical Information

Arles is easily accessible from major cities in Provence. If you're arriving by train, the Arles Train Station (Avenue Paulin Talabot, 13200 Arles, France) is a short walk from the city center. For those driving, there are several parking options available, including the Parking des Lices (Boulevard des Lices, 13200 Arles, France), which offers affordable rates.

3.5 Avignon: City of Popes and Palaces

Avignon, nestled along the banks of the Rhone River, boasts a rich history steeped in papal influence and architectural marvels. As you disembark your cruise and step onto Avignon's cobblestone streets, prepare to be transported back in time to an era of grandeur and cultural significance.

3.5.1 Palais des Papes: A Majestic UNESCO World Heritage Site

Nestled in the heart of Avignon, the Palais des Papes (Palace of the Popes) stands as one of the most impressive Gothic buildings in Europe and a symbol of the city's rich history. This formidable structure, once the residence of several pontiffs during the 14th century, has been a UNESCO World Heritage Site since 1995. Visiting the Palais des Papes is an immersive journey into the past, offering a glimpse into the lives of the popes who resided here and the historical events that shaped Avignon.

Historical Significance and Architectural Grandeur

The Palais des Papes was constructed between 1335 and 1370 during the Avignon Papacy when the Popes moved from Rome to Avignon due to political instability. The palace is divided into two main sections: the Old Palace (Palais Vieux) built by Benedict XII and the New Palace (Palais Neuf) built by Clement VI. The combined structure covers approximately 15,000 square meters, making it the largest Gothic palace in Europe.

The architectural style of the palace is a masterpiece of Gothic design. Its high, crenellated walls, massive towers, and fortified battlements give it the appearance of a fortress, while the intricate details of its interiors reflect the grandeur and opulence of the papal court. Visitors can marvel at the

Great Chapel, the Consistory Hall, and the private papal apartments, all adorned with frescoes by Italian artist Matteo Giovannetti.

Exploring the Interior

Upon entering the Palais des Papes, you will be greeted by the imposing Cour d'Honneur (Courtyard of Honor), which sets the stage for the grandeur that lies within. The interior of the palace is a labyrinth of grand halls, chapels, and private chambers, each offering a unique glimpse into the life and times of the papal court.

1. The Grand Chapel

The Grand Chapel, also known as the Great Chapel or the Chapel of Saint Martial, is one of the most awe-inspiring parts of the palace. This vast space, with its ribbed vaulted ceiling and soaring columns, was used for important religious ceremonies and gatherings. The chapel's acoustics are remarkable, making it a popular venue for concerts and musical performances today.

2. The Consistory Hall

The Consistory Hall, where the Pope held meetings with cardinals and high-ranking officials, is another highlight of the Palais des Papes. The hall is notable for its impressive frescoes, which depict scenes from the lives of saints and various biblical stories. These frescoes were meticulously restored to their original splendor, providing visitors with a vivid representation of medieval religious art.

3. Private Papal Apartments

The private apartments of the popes are perhaps the most intimate and fascinating parts of the palace. These rooms were not only living quarters but also served as places for prayer, reflection, and administrative work. The walls of the papal apartments are adorned with beautifully preserved frescoes by Matteo Giovannetti, depicting religious and pastoral scenes. One of the most famous rooms is the Pope's Bedchamber, where visitors can see the intricately painted ceiling and walls that create an almost magical atmosphere.

Cost and Accessibility

1. Admission Fees

The cost of admission to the Palais des Papes typically ranges from $12 to $16 per person. Discounts are available for seniors, students, and children under a certain age. There are also family tickets and group rates, making it more affordable for larger parties. Tickets can be purchased online in advance or at the entrance of the palace. It's advisable to check the official website for the latest prices and available discounts.

2. Opening Hours

The Palais des Papes is open daily, but the hours vary depending on the season. During the peak tourist season (typically from April to October), the palace is open from 9:00 AM to 7:00 PM. In the off-season, the hours are usually from 10:00 AM to 5:00 PM. It's a good idea to visit early in the morning or later in the afternoon to avoid the crowds and enjoy a more relaxed experience.

3. Guided Tours and Audio Guides

For a more in-depth exploration of the Palais des Papes, consider joining a guided tour. Knowledgeable guides provide fascinating insights into the history, architecture, and significance of the palace, bringing the stories of the popes and the medieval period to life. Guided tours are available in several languages and typically last about 90 minutes.

Alternatively, audio guides are available for rent at the entrance. These guides offer detailed commentary on various parts of the palace and allow you to explore at your own pace. The audio guides are available in multiple languages and are an excellent option for those who prefer a self-guided experience.

Tips for Visiting

1. Beat the Crowds

To make the most of your visit to the Palais des Papes, consider arriving early in the morning when the palace first opens or later in the afternoon. This way, you can avoid the peak hours when the palace is most crowded and enjoy a more leisurely exploration.

2. Dress Comfortably

The Palais des Papes is a large and sprawling complex, so be sure to wear comfortable shoes and clothing. The stone floors and staircases can be challenging to navigate, so sturdy footwear is recommended. Additionally, the interiors of the palace can be cool, even in the summer, so bringing a light jacket or sweater is advisable.

3. Plan Your Visit

The Palais des Papes is an extensive site with many rooms and halls to explore. To make the most of your visit, plan your route in advance and prioritize the areas that interest you the most. The official website of the Palais des Papes offers maps and suggested itineraries to help you plan your visit.

4. Photography

Photography is allowed in most areas of the Palais des Papes, but the use of flash is generally prohibited to protect the delicate frescoes and artworks. Be sure to check the signs and guidelines in each room. Capturing the intricate details of the architecture and decorations will provide you with lasting memories of your visit.

Dining and Refreshments

After exploring the Palais des Papes, you might want to relax and enjoy a meal or refreshment. There are several cafes and restaurants within walking distance of the palace, offering a range of dining options from quick snacks to full meals. Many establishments offer outdoor seating, allowing you to enjoy the charming atmosphere of Avignon while savoring local cuisine.

Nearby Attractions

While the Palais des Papes is undoubtedly the highlight of Avignon, there are several other attractions nearby that are worth visiting. The Pont Saint-Bénézet, or the Bridge of

Avignon, is just a short walk away and offers stunning views of the Rhone River and the city. The Rocher des Doms, a picturesque park situated on a hilltop, provides panoramic views of Avignon and the surrounding countryside.

Accessibility

The Palais des Papes is committed to being accessible to all visitors. There are ramps and elevators available to assist those with mobility issues, and the staff is trained to provide support and assistance as needed. Accessible restrooms are also available on-site. For visitors with visual or hearing impairments, audio guides with descriptive content and written materials are available.

Practical Information

1. Location and Contact Information

The Palais des Papes is located at Place du Palais, 84000 Avignon, France.

2. Amenities

The Palais des Papes offers several amenities to enhance your visit, including a gift shop where you can purchase souvenirs, books, and local products. There are also restrooms available for visitors. If you're traveling with young children, strollers are allowed in most areas of the palace, and baby-changing facilities are available.

3.5.2 Pont Saint-Bénézet: The Famous Bridge of Avignon

The Pont Saint-Bénézet, also affectionately known as the Pont d'Avignon, is one of the most iconic landmarks in Avignon. This medieval bridge, which once spanned the

Rhone River in its entirety, now stands partially ruined, evoking the charm and mystery of bygone centuries. Its enduring legacy, celebrated in the famous French children's song "Sur le Pont d'Avignon," continues to captivate the hearts of visitors from around the globe.

Historical Significance

Built between 1177 and 1185, the Pont Saint-Bénézet originally featured 22 arches and stretched an impressive 900 meters across the Rhone River. According to legend, the bridge was inspired by a shepherd named Bénézet, who claimed to have received divine instructions to construct a bridge in Avignon. Skeptical of his vision, the town's leaders were convinced when Bénézet miraculously lifted an enormous stone, proving the legitimacy of his mission.

The bridge played a crucial role in the medieval period, facilitating trade and travel between the city of Avignon and the opposite bank of the Rhone. It also served as a strategic military crossing, linking the Kingdom of France with the Papal territories. Over the centuries, however, the Rhone's powerful currents and frequent flooding took their toll, and by the 17th century, much of the bridge had collapsed. Today, only four of the original arches remain, standing as a poignant reminder of the bridge's storied past.

Architectural Features

Despite its ruined state, the Pont Saint-Bénézet offers a fascinating glimpse into medieval engineering and architecture. The remaining arches are constructed from a mix of limestone and local stone, showcasing the craftsmanship and ingenuity of the builders. The bridge's distinctive design, with its pointed arches and sturdy piers, reflects the Gothic architectural style that was prevalent during the time of its construction.

One of the most notable features of the Pont Saint-Bénézet is the small chapel of Saint Nicholas, which is perched on one of the bridge's piers. This charming Romanesque chapel, dedicated to the patron saint of boatmen, adds to the bridge's allure and provides a unique vantage point from which to admire the surrounding landscape. Visitors can step inside the chapel to see its simple yet elegant interior, complete with stone carvings and religious iconography.

Exploring the Pont Saint-Bénézet

A visit to the Pont Saint-Bénézet is a must for anyone traveling to Avignon. Whether you're a history enthusiast, an architecture buff, or simply looking to experience one of the city's most picturesque spots, the bridge offers something for everyone.

1. Cost and Accessibility

Access to the Pont Saint-Bénézet is included in the combined ticket for the Palais des Papes and the bridge, which costs approximately $12 to $16 per person. This ticket not only grants you entry to the bridge but also to one of Avignon's other major attractions, making it a great value for visitors looking to explore the city's rich history.

For those who wish to visit the bridge independently, separate tickets are available for around $5 to $8 per person. Children, students, and seniors often qualify for discounted rates, so be sure to inquire about available concessions when purchasing your tickets.

The bridge is generally open year-round, with opening hours varying depending on the season. During the peak tourist season (April to October), the bridge is typically open from 9:00 AM to 7:00 PM. In the off-season (November to March), the hours may be reduced, so it's advisable to check the official website or contact the tourist office for the most up-to-date information.

2. Guided Tours and Audio Guides

To enhance your visit, consider joining a guided tour or renting an audio guide. Guided tours are led by knowledgeable local experts who can provide fascinating insights into the bridge's history, architecture, and legends. These tours often include visits to other nearby attractions, offering a comprehensive overview of Avignon's rich cultural heritage.

Audio guides are available in multiple languages and can be rented for a small fee. They provide a detailed commentary on the bridge's history and significance, allowing you to explore at your own pace. The audio guides are easy to use and offer an immersive experience that brings the stories of the Pont Saint-Bénézet to life.

3. Photography and Scenic Views

The Pont Saint-Bénézet is a photographer's dream, with its picturesque arches and stunning views of the Rhone River and the Avignon skyline. Whether you're an amateur shutterbug or a seasoned professional, you'll find plenty of opportunities to capture beautiful shots of this iconic landmark.

For the best photos, visit the bridge early in the morning or late in the afternoon, when the soft light creates a magical atmosphere. The golden hour, just after sunrise and before sunset, is particularly ideal for photography, as the warm hues highlight the textures and details of the stonework.

Don't forget to take advantage of the various viewpoints around the bridge. The banks of the Rhone River offer excellent perspectives, allowing you to frame the bridge against the backdrop of the river and the city. For a unique angle, consider taking a boat tour that passes beneath the bridge, providing a different vantage point from which to appreciate its architectural beauty.

Local Legends and Folklore

The Pont Saint-Bénézet is steeped in legends and folklore that add to its allure. According to one popular tale, the bridge was constructed by angels who assisted Bénézet in his divine mission. Another story tells of a young shepherdess who danced on the bridge every night, enchanting passersby with her grace and beauty.

These legends have inspired countless artists, writers, and musicians over the centuries. The famous children's song "Sur le Pont d'Avignon" is perhaps the most well-known cultural reference, depicting the joy and merriment of dancing on the bridge. This charming melody has been passed down through generations, keeping the spirit of the Pont Saint-Bénézet alive in the hearts of many.

3.5.3 Cultural Experiences: Festivals, Museums, and Performances

Avignon's cultural scene is a highlight of any Rhone River cruise. Here, we'll explore the must-visit cultural attractions and events that make Avignon a standout destination.

Festivals in Avignon

1. Avignon Theatre Festival (Festival d'Avignon)

The Avignon Theatre Festival is one of the most prestigious and oldest theater festivals in the world. Founded in 1947 by Jean Vilar, it transforms Avignon into a bustling stage every July, attracting theater enthusiasts, performers, and artists from around the globe.

Highlights:

Main Program (In): Featuring high-profile productions by renowned directors and companies, often staged in historical venues such as the Courtyard of the Palais des Papes.

Off Program (Off): Showcases a diverse array of performances, from avant-garde theater to experimental works, across various smaller venues and outdoor spaces in the city.

Cost: Tickets for main program performances typically range from $20 to $80, depending on the show and seating category. Off program performances are generally more affordable, with prices averaging $10 to $30.

Tip: Book tickets in advance, especially for popular shows in the main program. Many performances sell out quickly, and purchasing early ensures you secure a spot.

2. Les Hivernales Dance Festival

Held every February, Les Hivernales Dance Festival celebrates contemporary dance with a dynamic lineup of performances, workshops, and masterclasses. It provides a platform for both emerging and established choreographers to showcase their work.

Highlights:

Performances: Features a mix of international and French dance companies presenting innovative and thought-provoking works.

Workshops: Offers dance enthusiasts the opportunity to participate in classes led by professional dancers and choreographers.

Cost: Performance tickets typically cost between $15 and $40. Workshop fees vary depending on the duration and instructor but generally range from $50 to $150.

Tip: Participate in a workshop to gain a deeper appreciation of contemporary dance and perhaps even learn a few moves yourself.

Museums in Avignon

1. Musée Calvet

Housed in an 18th-century mansion, the Musée Calvet is Avignon's premier fine arts museum. It boasts an impressive collection of paintings, sculptures, decorative arts, and archaeological artifacts.

Highlights:

Art Collections: Features works from the Middle Ages to the 20th century, including pieces by renowned artists such as Joseph Vernet and Simon de Châlons.

Decorative Arts: Displays fine examples of furniture, ceramics, and textiles from various historical periods.

Archaeology: Exhibits artifacts from ancient civilizations, including Roman, Greek, and Egyptian relics.

Cost: General admission is around $10, with discounted rates for students and seniors. Children under 18 often enjoy free entry.

Hours: Open Tuesday to Sunday, 10:00 AM to 6:00 PM. Closed on Mondays and certain public holidays.

Tip: Plan your visit in the late afternoon when the museum is less crowded, allowing for a more intimate experience with the artworks.

2. Musée Angladon

The Musée Angladon offers an eclectic collection of art spanning several centuries, housed in a charming 18th-century mansion. It was founded by the heirs of the artist Jean-Baptiste Angladon and his wife, who were passionate art collectors.

Highlights:

Impressionist and Post-Impressionist Art: Features works by masters such as Van Gogh, Cézanne, Degas, and Modigliani.

18th and 19th Century Art: Showcases pieces from various European schools, including Italian, Flemish, and French artists.

Decorative Arts and Furniture: Presents exquisite examples of period furniture, objets d'art, and fashion from the 18th and 19th centuries.

Cost: Admission is typically $8, with reduced rates for students, seniors, and groups. Children under 12 may enter for free.

Hours: Open Tuesday to Sunday, 1:00 PM to 6:00 PM. Closed on Mondays and certain public holidays.

Tip: Take advantage of the free audio guide available at the museum to enrich your visit with detailed information about the artworks and their historical context.

3. Collection Lambert

The Collection Lambert is a contemporary art museum housed in two historical hôtels particuliers. It showcases the impressive private collection of art dealer Yvon Lambert, featuring works from the 1960s to the present day.

Highlights:

Contemporary Art: Includes pieces by prominent contemporary artists such as Anselm Kiefer, Jean-Michel Basquiat, and Sol LeWitt.

Temporary Exhibitions: Hosts rotating exhibitions that explore various themes and artistic movements.

Public Programs: Offers a range of educational activities, including artist talks, workshops, and guided tours.

Cost: General admission is around $12, with discounts for students, seniors, and children. Special exhibitions may have additional fees.

Hours: Open Tuesday to Sunday, 11:00 AM to 6:00 PM. Closed on Mondays.

Tip: Visit on the first Sunday of the month when admission is free, allowing you to explore the museum's extensive collection at no cost.

Performances in Avignon

1. Opéra Grand Avignon

The Opéra Grand Avignon is a cultural gem that hosts a variety of performances, including opera, ballet, and classical concerts. The opera house itself is an architectural marvel, featuring an elegant interior and excellent acoustics.

Highlights:

Opera Performances: Features classic operas by composers such as Verdi, Puccini, and Mozart, performed by talented international and local artists.

Ballet: Showcases productions by prestigious ballet companies, offering a mix of classical and contemporary dance.

Concerts: Hosts orchestral and chamber music concerts, often featuring renowned musicians and conductors.

Cost: Ticket prices vary depending on the performance and seating category, ranging from $30 to $120. Discounts are often available for students, seniors, and groups.

Hours: Performance times vary, with most evening shows starting around 8:00 PM. Matinee performances are also offered on weekends.

Tip: Dress appropriately for an evening at the opera. While formal attire is not mandatory, smart casual is generally recommended.

2. Théâtre des Halles

Located in the heart of Avignon, the Théâtre des Halles is known for its diverse program of theatrical performances. It offers a mix of contemporary and classic plays, often featuring innovative and thought-provoking productions.

Highlights:

Theatrical Productions: Presents a range of genres, from drama and comedy to experimental theater.

Festivals: Hosts various theater festivals throughout the year, providing a platform for emerging playwrights and directors.

Workshops and Readings: Offers opportunities for theater enthusiasts to engage with the creative process through workshops, readings, and discussions.

Cost: Ticket prices generally range from $15 to $40, depending on the production and seating. Discounts are available for students, seniors, and groups.

Hours: Performance times vary, with evening shows typically starting at 8:00 PM. Matinee performances are often scheduled on weekends and during festivals.

Tip: Arrive early to explore the theater's charming courtyard and enjoy a pre-show drink or snack.

3. Avignon Jazz Festival

Held annually in August, the Avignon Jazz Festival is a must-visit for music lovers. It features a lineup of international jazz artists performing in various venues across the city, from intimate clubs to outdoor stages.

Highlights:

Live Performances: Showcases a mix of traditional and contemporary jazz, with performances by both established artists and rising stars.

Workshops and Masterclasses: Offers music enthusiasts the chance to learn from professional musicians through interactive sessions.

Jam Sessions: Provides opportunities for musicians to collaborate and improvise in a relaxed, informal setting.

Cost: Ticket prices for individual performances typically range from $20 to $50. Festival passes, which grant access to multiple shows, are available for around $100 to $200.

Hours: Performance times vary, with evening shows usually starting at 9:00 PM. Some venues also host late-night jam sessions.

Tip: Purchase a festival pass for the best value and access to a wide range of performances and events.

3.5.4 Shopping in Avignon: Markets and Boutiques
The Markets of Avignon

1. Les Halles d'Avignon

- Address: Place Pie, 84000 Avignon
- Hours: Tuesday to Sunday, 6:00 AM to 2:00 PM

Les Halles d'Avignon is a bustling covered market that serves as the heart of the city's food culture. Here, you'll find an impressive array of fresh produce, meats, cheeses, and other gourmet delights. The market is a sensory overload with the sights, sounds, and scents of Provence.

What to Buy:

- Local Produce: Seasonal fruits and vegetables from local farms.
- Cheeses: A variety of regional cheeses, including creamy goat cheeses and tangy Roquefort.
- Olives and Olive Oil: High-quality products that capture the essence of Provence.

- Herbs de Provence: A fragrant blend of dried herbs perfect for cooking.

Tip: Visit on Saturday mornings when the market is at its liveliest, and many vendors offer free samples.

2. Place des Carmes Market

- Address: Place des Carmes, 84000 Avignon
- Hours: Saturdays, 7:00 AM to 1:00 PM

The Place des Carmes Market is a smaller, more intimate market compared to Les Halles. It's the perfect place to experience the local ambiance and discover handmade goods and fresh local produce.

What to Buy:

- Flowers: Beautiful bouquets and potted plants.
- Artisanal Bread: Freshly baked bread from local bakeries.
- Handicrafts: Unique handmade items, such as pottery and textiles.

Tip: Arrive early to get the best selection of fresh flowers and baked goods.

3. Brocante Market

- Address: Allées de l'Oulle, 84000 Avignon
- Hours: First Saturday of every month, 8:00 AM to 6:00 PM

For those who love antiques and vintage items, the Brocante Market is a must-visit. Held monthly, this market features an eclectic mix of antiques, collectibles, and vintage goods.

What to Buy:

- Antiques: Furniture, decor, and unique pieces with historical significance.
- Vintage Clothing: Retro fashion items from different eras.
- Books and Records: Old books, vinyl records, and other media.

Tip: Bargain hunting is encouraged, so don't be afraid to negotiate prices with vendors.

Boutiques in Avignon

1. L'Artisan Parfumeur

- Address: 19 Rue de la République, 84000 Avignon
- Hours: Monday to Saturday, 10:00 AM to 7:00 PM

L'Artisan Parfumeur is a boutique dedicated to the art of perfume making. Here, you can find exquisite fragrances crafted with high-quality ingredients, each telling its own story.

What to Buy:

- Perfumes: Unique scents created by master perfumers.
- Candles: Scented candles that evoke the essence of Provence.
- Gift Sets: Beautifully packaged sets perfect for souvenirs or gifts.

Tip: Ask for a fragrance consultation to find a scent that perfectly matches your preferences.

2. La Maison du Savon de Marseille

- Address: 20 Rue Saint-Agricol, 84000 Avignon
- Hours: Monday to Saturday, 10:00 AM to 7:00 PM

La Maison du Savon de Marseille specializes in traditional Marseille soap and other natural body care products. This boutique is a haven for those seeking high-quality, handcrafted soaps.

What to Buy:

- Marseille Soap: Authentic, natural soaps made with olive oil.
- Bath Products: Luxurious bath salts and oils.
- Skin Care: Natural lotions and creams.

Tip: Take advantage of in-store promotions and bulk discounts on soaps and bath products.

3. La Fromagerie de l'Isle

- Address: 4 Rue de la Petite Fusterie, 84000 Avignon
- Hours: Tuesday to Saturday, 9:30 AM to 1:00 PM and 4:00 PM to 7:00 PM

La Fromagerie de l'Isle is a cheese lover's paradise, offering a wide selection of cheeses from the region and beyond. The knowledgeable staff can help you choose the perfect cheese for any occasion.

What to Buy:

- Regional Cheeses: Varieties such as Comté, Reblochon, and Beaufort.
- Specialty Cheeses: Unique and rare cheeses not found elsewhere.
- Accompaniments: Pair your cheese with local honey, jams, and crackers.

Tip: Don't hesitate to ask for samples to ensure you pick the cheeses that best suit your taste.

4. Côté Sud

- Address: 26 Rue des Fourbisseurs, 84000 Avignon
- Hours: Monday to Saturday, 10:00 AM to 7:00 PM

Côté Sud offers a curated selection of home decor and lifestyle products inspired by the Provencal way of life. This boutique is perfect for finding stylish and unique items to bring a touch of Provence to your home.

What to Buy:

- Home Decor: Beautiful table linens, ceramics, and glassware.
- Kitchen Accessories: High-quality kitchen tools and gadgets.
- Gifts: Thoughtful gifts such as scented candles and artisanal jams.

Tip: Check out their seasonal sales for great deals on selected items.

CHAPTER FOUR
DINING AND CUISINE ALONG THE RHONE

4.1 Gastronomic Highlights: Regional Specialties and Delicacies

Embarking on a Rhone River cruise is not just a journey through stunning landscapes but also a culinary adventure through the heart of France. As you traverse the river, tantalizing your taste buds with the region's gastronomic treasures is an essential part of the experience. Here are some of the gastronomic highlights you simply can't miss:

1. Lyon: The Gastronomic Capital

Lyon, often hailed as the gastronomic capital of France, is a must-visit for any food lover. This vibrant city is known for its "bouchons," traditional bistros serving hearty, home-style dishes. These establishments are quintessentially Lyonnais and provide a genuine taste of local culture.

Must-Try Dishes in Lyon:

- Coq au Vin: A classic French dish where chicken is slow-cooked in red wine with mushrooms, onions, and bacon. It's rich and flavorful, typically served with potatoes or pasta. Expect to pay around $25 to $35 for this dish at a reputable bouchon.
- Quenelles de Brochet: These delicate pike fish dumplings are a Lyon specialty. They are often served with a creamy Nantua sauce, made from crayfish butter and cream. A serving will cost approximately $20 to $30.

- Salade Lyonnaise: A fresh salad of frisée lettuce, crispy bacon lardons, croutons, and a poached egg, all dressed in a tangy vinaigrette. This light yet flavorful dish is priced around $15 to $20.

Top Bouchons to Visit:

- Le Bouchon des Filles: Located at 20 Rue Sergent Blandan, this popular spot is known for its welcoming atmosphere and traditional dishes. Reservations are recommended. Prices range from $20 to $40 per person.
- Café Comptoir Abel: Situated at 25 Rue Guynemer, this historic bouchon dates back to 1928 and is famed for its authentic Lyonnaise cuisine. Expect to spend about $25 to $50 per person.

2. Avignon: Provencal Flavors

As your cruise reaches Avignon, the flavors of Provence will take center stage. This region is celebrated for its fresh ingredients, Mediterranean influences, and vibrant culinary scene.

Provencal Delicacies to Enjoy:

- Ratatouille: A colorful vegetable stew made with tomatoes, zucchini, eggplant, peppers, and onions, seasoned with herbs like thyme and basil. It's a vegetarian delight available for around $15 to $25.
- Bouillabaisse: Originating from Marseille but popular in Avignon, this traditional fish stew features a variety of seafood simmered with tomatoes, saffron, and herbs. Served with rouille sauce and crusty bread, this dish typically costs $30 to $50.

- Pissaladière: A savory tart topped with caramelized onions, anchovies, and olives, perfect for a light lunch or snack. You can enjoy this Provencal pizza for about $10 to $20.

Dining Spots in Avignon:

- La Fourchette: Found at 17 Rue Racine, this charming restaurant offers a delightful array of Provencal dishes. Prices range from $25 to $50 per person.
- L'Agape: Located at 21 Place des Corps Saints, L'Agape combines modern cuisine with traditional flavors, making it a must-visit for food enthusiasts. Expect to pay between $30 and $60 per person.

3. Tournon-sur-Rhône and Tain-l'Hermitage: Wine and Truffles

The twin towns of Tournon-sur-Rhône and Tain-l'Hermitage are a paradise for wine lovers and truffle enthusiasts. These regions are famed for their exceptional wines and truffle-rich landscapes.

Wine and Truffle Highlights:

- Truffle Hunting: Experience the thrill of hunting for truffles with a local expert and their trained dog. After the hunt, enjoy a truffle-themed meal, savoring the earthy, aromatic flavors of this prized delicacy. Truffle hunting experiences usually start at $100 per person.
- Wine Tasting: Visit the renowned vineyards of Tain-l'Hermitage, where you can taste some of the best wines in the Northern Rhone Valley. Look for full-bodied Syrahs and elegant Viogniers. Wine tasting sessions typically cost around $20 to $50 per person.

Top Wineries and Truffle Spots:

- Cave de Tain: Located at 22 Route de Larnage, Tain-l'Hermitage, this winery offers guided tours and tastings. Prices vary depending on the tasting package.
- Maison Gambert: Another excellent spot for wine lovers, situated at 12 Avenue Ozier, Tain-l'Hermitage. Enjoy a comprehensive tasting experience for about $30 per person.

4. Arles: Inspired by Van Gogh

Arles, with its rich history and artistic heritage, also boasts a delightful culinary scene influenced by the flavors of Provence and the Camargue region.

Culinary Specialties in Arles:

- Gardianne de Taureau: A traditional stew made from bull meat, marinated in red wine and slow-cooked with onions, garlic, and herbs. This hearty dish reflects the rustic charm of the Camargue. Prices range from $25 to $40.
- Fougasse: A type of flatbread often flavored with olives, herbs, and sometimes cheese. It's a perfect snack or accompaniment to a meal, costing around $5 to $10.
- Navettes d'Arles: These boat-shaped biscuits flavored with orange blossom water are a sweet treat from the region. You can find them for about $5 to $10 per pack.

Notable Restaurants in Arles:

- L'Atelier de Jean-Luc Rabanel: Located at 7 Rue des Carmes, this Michelin-starred restaurant offers a gourmet experience with a focus on local, organic ingredients. Expect to spend around $100 to $200 per person for a tasting menu.

- Le Cilantro: At 31 Rue Porte de Laure, this restaurant provides a creative take on Provencal cuisine, blending traditional and contemporary flavors. Prices range from $30 to $60 per person.

5. Viviers: Medieval Charm and Modern Flavors

Viviers, a quaint medieval town, offers a serene backdrop for culinary exploration. Here, you can enjoy both traditional and modern interpretations of regional dishes.

Culinary Delights in Viviers:

- Caillette: A rustic terrine made from pork, herbs, and greens, often served with fresh bread and pickles. It's a hearty starter available for about $10 to $20.
- Chevreton: Local goat cheese that pairs perfectly with a glass of Rhone Valley wine. Enjoy this creamy delicacy for around $5 to $15.
- Raviole de Romans: Tiny pasta pockets filled with cheese and herbs, originating from the nearby town of Romans-sur-Isère. A delicious serving can be found for $15 to $25.

Recommended Dining in Viviers:

- Le Relais du Vivarais: Situated at 5 Quai Jules Roche, this riverside restaurant offers traditional French cuisine with stunning views of the Rhone. Prices range from $25 to $50 per person..
- Auberge de l'Helvie: Located at Place de la République, this cozy eatery serves regional

specialties in a charming medieval setting. Expect to pay between $20 and $40 per person..

4.2 Dining Options Onboard: From Gourmet Meals to Casual Fare

Gourmet Dining in the Main Restaurant

The main restaurant on most Rhone River cruise ships is where you'll find the pinnacle of onboard dining. This is where talented chefs showcase their skills, preparing multi-course meals that highlight both regional specialties and international cuisine. Here's what makes dining in the main restaurant a highlight of your cruise:

- Regional Specialties: One of the joys of cruising along the Rhone is the opportunity to sample the local cuisine without ever leaving the ship. Expect dishes such as coq au vin, boeuf bourguignon, and duck à l'orange, all prepared with fresh, locally sourced ingredients. The chefs often take inspiration from the regions you are cruising through, ensuring an authentic culinary experience.
- International Cuisine: While regional specialties take center stage, the main restaurant also offers a variety of international dishes to cater to diverse palates. From Italian pasta to Asian stir-fries, there's something to satisfy every craving.
- Wine Pairings: Dining in the main restaurant is often accompanied by an extensive wine list featuring selections from the Rhone Valley and beyond. Knowledgeable sommeliers are on hand to recommend the perfect wine to complement your meal. A glass of Châteauneuf-du-Pape with your duck

confit, or a crisp Viognier with your fish course, can elevate the dining experience to new heights.

- Ambiance and Service: The ambiance in the main restaurant is typically elegant, with white tablecloths, fine china, and attentive service. The waitstaff are trained to provide a high level of service, ensuring that your dining experience is both relaxing and enjoyable. Dinner is often a formal affair, providing an opportunity to dress up and enjoy a sophisticated evening.

- Cost and Inclusions: Dinner in the main restaurant is usually included in the cost of your cruise fare, although premium wine selections and certain specialty dishes may incur an additional charge. It's always a good idea to check with your cruise line for specific details.

Casual Dining at the Bistro or Café

For those times when you prefer a more relaxed dining experience, the onboard bistro or café offers a variety of casual options. Here's what you can expect:

- Light Meals and Snacks: The bistro or café is perfect for grabbing a quick bite or enjoying a light meal. Options typically include salads, sandwiches, soups, and pastries. It's an ideal spot for a leisurely lunch or an afternoon snack between excursions.

- Flexibility and Convenience: One of the advantages of casual dining options is the flexibility they offer. Unlike the main restaurant, which often has set dining times, the bistro or café may be open throughout the day, allowing you to dine at your convenience. This is particularly useful if you return from a shore excursion later than expected or if you simply prefer a more flexible dining schedule.

- Outdoor Seating: Many river cruise ships offer outdoor seating options at the bistro or café, allowing you to enjoy your meal while taking in the scenic views. Dining alfresco on the sun deck is a delightful way to experience the passing landscapes, from rolling vineyards to charming riverside villages.

- Informal Atmosphere: The atmosphere in the bistro or café is generally more informal and relaxed than the main restaurant. It's a great place to unwind with a cup of coffee or a glass of wine and socialize with fellow passengers in a laid-back setting.

- Cost and Inclusions: Casual dining options are typically included in your cruise fare, making it easy to enjoy a variety of meals without worrying about additional costs. Be sure to check your cruise line's policies to understand what's included and if there are any extra charges for certain items.

Alfresco Dining on the Sun Deck

Dining alfresco on the sun deck is one of the most delightful ways to enjoy your meals while cruising the Rhone River. Here's why this option is so popular:

- Scenic Views: The sun deck offers unparalleled views of the surrounding landscapes. Whether you're enjoying breakfast as the sun rises over the river or savoring a sunset dinner, the ever-changing scenery provides a stunning backdrop for your meal. Picture yourself dining amidst the vineyards of Tain-l'Hermitage or the medieval architecture of Avignon – it's an experience you won't forget.

- Freshly Grilled Specialties: Many river cruise ships feature outdoor grills on the sun deck, where chefs prepare a variety of freshly grilled dishes. From succulent steaks to grilled vegetables and seafood, the aroma of sizzling food adds to the ambiance. It's a casual yet delicious dining option that's perfect for a warm, sunny day.
- Relaxed Atmosphere: Alfresco dining on the sun deck is generally more relaxed and informal than dining in the main restaurant. It's an ideal setting for a leisurely meal with friends or family, accompanied by the gentle breeze and the sounds of the river. The informal setting encourages socializing and enjoying the natural beauty of the surroundings.
- Open-Air Bar: Many sun decks also feature an open-air bar where you can enjoy a refreshing drink with your meal. Whether it's a glass of local wine, a cocktail, or a cold beer, the open-air bar adds to the relaxed and enjoyable atmosphere.
- Cost and Inclusions: Like other dining options, alfresco dining on the sun deck is usually included in the cost of your cruise fare. However, it's a good idea to check if there are any special events or premium menu items that might incur additional charges.

Specialty Dining Experiences

For those looking to elevate their culinary journey, many Rhone River cruise lines offer specialty dining experiences. These exclusive events provide a unique opportunity to indulge in extraordinary meals and culinary activities. Here's what you can look forward to:

- Themed Dinners: Specialty themed dinners are a highlight of many river cruises. These events often feature menus inspired by a particular region or culinary tradition. For example, you might enjoy a Provencal-themed dinner with dishes like bouillabaisse and ratatouille, accompanied by live music and traditional decor. Themed dinners provide a fun and immersive way to experience the local culture and cuisine.

- Wine Pairing Events: For wine enthusiasts, wine pairing events are a must. These dinners feature expertly curated wine selections paired with each course, enhancing the flavors and textures of the dishes. A sommelier will guide you through the tasting, explaining the nuances of each wine and how it complements the food. Wine pairing events are often held in intimate settings, providing a personalized and educational experience.

- Chef's Table Dinners: The Chef's Table is a special dining experience where a limited number of guests are treated to a multi-course meal prepared by the ship's head chef. This exclusive event typically features gourmet dishes that showcase the chef's creativity and expertise, using the finest ingredients available. Guests often have the opportunity to interact with the chef, gaining insight into the preparation and inspiration behind each dish. Chef's Table dinners usually come with an additional charge and require advance reservations due to limited seating.

- Cooking Demonstrations and Classes: Some river cruise lines offer cooking demonstrations and classes as part of their specialty dining experiences. These events allow you to learn from the ship's chefs or guest chefs, gaining hands-on experience in preparing local dishes. Whether you're mastering the art of making French pastries or learning the secrets of a perfect Provencal stew, cooking classes are both educational and entertaining. Prices for cooking classes vary, but they typically range from $50 to $100 per person.

- Private Dining: For a truly exclusive experience, some cruise lines offer private dining options. Whether it's a romantic dinner for two or a special celebration with friends, private dining provides a personalized and intimate setting. You can often choose from a selection of gourmet menus, and the meal is typically served in a private dining room or a secluded area of the ship. Private dining experiences usually come with a premium price tag, but they offer a unique and memorable way to celebrate a special occasion.

Participating in specialty dining experiences allows you to delve deeper into the culinary traditions of the Rhone River region and enjoy unique and memorable meals. Be sure to check with your cruise line for specific details on the specialty dining options available and make reservations early to secure your spot.

4.3 Culinary Experiences Ashore: Farm Visits, Cooking Classes, and Food Tours

One of the joys of exploring the Rhone River region is the opportunity to immerse yourself in its culinary culture through a variety of unique experiences ashore. From visiting local farms to mastering French cooking techniques in a hands-on class, there's something for every food enthusiast to enjoy. Here are some culinary experiences you won't want to miss:

Farm Visits in Provence

One of the highlights of a Rhone River cruise is the chance to visit the idyllic farms of Provence. These visits offer a firsthand look at traditional farming practices and the production of local specialties.

1. Olive Farms: Provence is famous for its olives and olive oil. Visiting an olive farm allows you to witness the olive harvesting process and learn about oil production. At places like Moulin Castelas (Vallon des Glauges, 13520 Les Baux-de-Provence, France), you can take a guided tour of the groves, observe the pressing process, and sample a variety of olive oils. Many tours also include a tasting session, where you can compare different oils and learn about their distinct flavors. Prices for farm visits range from $20 to $50 per person, depending on the activities included.

2. Lavender Farms: The sight and scent of lavender fields are quintessentially Provencal. Visiting a lavender farm, such as Distillerie Les Coulets (Route de Nyons, 26770 Montbrun-les-Bains, France), during the blooming season (typically late June to August) offers a sensory delight. Learn about the cultivation and harvesting of lavender, and see how it is distilled into essential oils. Many farms also produce lavender-infused products like honey, soaps, and sachets, which make perfect souvenirs.

3. Truffle Farms: Truffle hunting is a unique and exciting experience that you can enjoy in Tournon-sur-Rhône. Join a local truffle hunter and their trained dog for a foray into the countryside in search of these prized fungi. After the hunt, you'll be treated to a truffle-themed meal, highlighting the earthy flavors of freshly harvested truffles. Companies like Les Truffières de la Côte (26150 Die, France) offer such experiences, typically priced around $100 per person.

Visiting these farms not only provides insight into local agriculture but also allows you to taste the freshest produce and products straight from the source.

Cooking Classes in Lyon

Lyon, often referred to as the gastronomic capital of France, is the perfect place to enhance your culinary skills. The city's vibrant food scene and rich culinary heritage make it an ideal setting for cooking classes.

1. Les Halles de Lyon Paul Bocuse: Named after the legendary chef Paul Bocuse, this indoor market is a haven for food lovers. Participating in a cooking class here, such as those offered by L'Atelier des Chefs (Cours Lafayette, 69003 Lyon), gives you the chance to work with top-quality ingredients sourced directly from market vendors. Classes cover a range of topics, from classic French dishes to contemporary cuisine, and often include a market tour, hands-on cooking session, and a meal. Prices start at around $100 per person.

2. Plum Lyon Teaching Kitchen: This English-language cooking school offers intimate classes focusing on seasonal, market-driven cuisine. Located in the heart of Lyon (91 Quai Pierre Scize, 69005 Lyon, France), Plum Lyon Teaching Kitchen provides a relaxed and educational environment where you can learn to prepare traditional Lyonnaise dishes. Classes typically include a visit to a local market, where you'll select ingredients, followed by a hands-on cooking session and a shared meal. Prices for classes are around $150 per person.

3. In Cuisine: This cooking school offers a variety of classes, from pastry-making to gourmet cuisine. Located in Lyon's Presqu'île district (1 Place Bellecour, 69002 Lyon), In

Cuisine's classes are taught by professional chefs and provide a thorough understanding of French cooking techniques. Whether you're interested in baking delicate pastries or crafting elaborate main courses, you'll find a class that suits your interests. Prices vary, but most classes cost between $80 and $120 per person.

Participating in a cooking class in Lyon not only equips you with new culinary skills but also deepens your appreciation for the region's rich food culture.

Food Tours in Avignon

Exploring the historic city of Avignon through its food is an experience not to be missed. Guided food tours take you to the city's best markets, shops, and eateries, offering a taste of Provencal cuisine and culture.

1. Les Halles Market Tour: Les Halles is Avignon's bustling central market, filled with stalls offering fresh produce, meats, cheeses, and more. A guided tour of Les Halles, such as those offered by Provence Gourmet,takes you through the market's aisles, introducing you to local vendors and their specialties. You'll sample a variety of foods, from charcuterie and cheeses to pastries and sweets, while learning about the ingredients and culinary traditions of Provence. Tours typically last around 2-3 hours and cost between $50 and $80 per person.

2. Provence and Wine Food Tours: This company offers walking food tours that combine tastings with cultural insights. Explore Avignon's historic center while sampling local delicacies like tapenade, nougat, and macarons. Each stop offers a chance to taste something new and learn about the history and significance of the food. Provence and Wine Food Tours also include visits to wine shops, where you can

sample regional wines and learn about the winemaking process. Prices for tours range from $60 to $100 per person.

3. Taste of Provence Walking Tour: This tour offers a comprehensive look at Avignon's food scene, combining visits to markets, bakeries, and specialty shops. You'll enjoy tastings of local cheeses, meats, pastries, and more, while your guide shares stories and insights about Provencal cuisine. Taste of Provence Walking Tours typically last around 3 hours and cost approximately $70 per person.

Joining a food tour in Avignon allows you to discover the city's culinary treasures, meet local producers, and enjoy a variety of delicious tastings.

Wine Tasting in Tain-l'Hermitage

Tain-l'Hermitage is renowned for its exceptional wines, making it a must-visit destination for wine enthusiasts. Wine tasting experiences in this charming town provide an opportunity to explore the local vineyards and sample world-class wines.

1. Maison M. Chapoutier: This historic winery offers a range of tasting experiences, from introductory tastings to in-depth tours of the vineyards. Located at 18 Avenue Dr Paul Durand, 26600 Tain-l'Hermitage, France, Maison M. Chapoutier provides guided tours that include visits to the cellars and vineyards, along with tastings of their acclaimed wines. Prices for tastings start at around $20 per person, with additional fees for more extensive tours and tastings.

2. Cave de Tain: This cooperative winery produces some of the best wines in the Northern Rhone Valley. Located at 22 Route de Larnage, 26600 Tain-l'Hermitage, France, Cave de Tain offers guided tours and tastings that showcase their diverse range of wines. Learn about the winemaking process,

explore the cellars, and enjoy a tasting session featuring wines like Crozes-Hermitage and Saint-Joseph. Prices for tours and tastings start at $15 per person.

3. Paul Jaboulet Aîné: Another prestigious winery in Tain-l'Hermitage, Paul Jaboulet Aîné offers a variety of wine tasting experiences. Located at 45 Avenue Dr Paul Durand, 26600 Tain-l'Hermitage, France, Paul Jaboulet Aîné provides tours that include visits to the vineyards and cellars, along with tastings of their renowned wines. Prices for tastings and tours start at $25 per person.

4. La Cité du Chocolat Valrhona: For a unique pairing experience, visit La Cité du Chocolat Valrhona (12 Avenue du Président Roosevelt, 26600 Tain-l'Hermitage, France). This chocolate museum offers tours that include wine and chocolate pairings, allowing you to explore the complementary flavors of fine wines and premium chocolates. Prices for wine and chocolate pairing experiences start at $30 per person.

Wine tasting in Tain-l'Hermitage provides a delightful way to discover the diverse terroirs and winemaking traditions of the Rhone Valley. Whether you're a seasoned oenophile or simply enjoy a good glass of wine, these tastings offer a memorable glimpse into the world of French viticulture.

CHAPTER FIVE
ACTIVITIES AND EXCURSIONS DURING YOUR RHONE RIVER CRUISE

5.1 Guided Tours: City Walks, Historic Sites, and Hidden Gems

Guided City Walks

1. Lyon

Lyon, the gastronomic capital of France, is a city rich in history and culture. A guided city walk through Vieux Lyon, the Renaissance district, is a must. This area is known for its narrow cobblestone streets, colorful buildings, and hidden traboules (covered passageways). Notable stops include the St. Jean Cathedral, a stunning example of Gothic architecture, and the Musée Gadagne, which houses the city's history and puppet museums. Guided tours in Lyon typically cost around $20 to $50 per person, depending on the length and depth of the tour.

- St. Jean Cathedral: Located at Place Saint-Jean, 69005 Lyon. Open daily from 8:00 AM to 7:00 PM. Entry is free.
- Musée Gadagne: Located at 1 Place du Petit Collège, 69005 Lyon. Open Wednesday to Sunday from 10:30 AM to 6:30 PM. Entry fee is $8.

2. Avignon

Avignon, known for its historical significance and architectural beauty, offers numerous guided tours that highlight its rich past. The Palais des Papes, a UNESCO

World Heritage site, is the largest Gothic palace in Europe and a symbol of the city's ecclesiastical history. Guided tours of the palace cost around $15 per person and last about two hours. Another must-see is the Pont d'Avignon, made famous by the song "Sur le Pont d'Avignon." Walking across this iconic bridge costs approximately $7 for adults.

- Palais des Papes: Located at Place du Palais, 84000 Avignon. Open daily from 10:00 AM to 6:00 PM. Entry fee is $15.
- Pont d'Avignon: Located at Boulevard de la Ligne, 84000 Avignon. Open daily from 9:00 AM to 7:00 PM. Entry fee is $7.

3. Arles

Arles, a town that inspired many of Vincent van Gogh's masterpieces, is filled with Roman and Romanesque monuments. A guided tour of the Arles Amphitheatre, a UNESCO World Heritage site, is essential for history enthusiasts. Entry is around $9, and guided tours are available for an additional fee. Another highlight is the Church of St. Trophime, with its stunning cloister.

- Arles Amphitheatre: Located at 1 Rond-Point des Arènes, 13200 Arles. Open daily from 9:00 AM to 7:00 PM. Entry fee is $9.
- Church of St. Trophime: Located at Place de la République, 13200 Arles. Open daily from 9:00 AM to 6:00 PM. Entry is free.

Historic Sites

1. Vienne

Vienne is a town with a rich Roman heritage. The Roman Theatre, one of the best-preserved in Europe, is a must-see.

A guided tour here costs about $10 and provides insight into the city's Roman past. Nearby, the Temple of Augustus and Livia, a Roman temple dating back to 10 BC, is free to visit and offers a glimpse into ancient religious practices.

- Roman Theatre: Located at Place Charles de Gaulle, 38200 Vienne. Open daily from 9:00 AM to 6:00 PM. Entry fee is $10.
- Temple of Augustus and Livia: Located at Place de l'Ancien Forum, 38200 Vienne. Open daily from 9:00 AM to 6:00 PM. Entry is free.

2. Tournon-sur-Rhône

Tournon-sur-Rhône, a picturesque town, is home to the historic Tournon Castle. This castle offers panoramic views of the river and surrounding vineyards. Entry is $6, and guided tours provide fascinating insights into the region's history. The castle also hosts a variety of exhibitions throughout the year.

Tournon Castle: Located at 14 Place Auguste Faure, 07300 Tournon-sur-Rhône. Open daily from 10:00 AM to 6:00 PM. Entry fee is $6.

3. Viviers

Viviers is a hidden gem known for its medieval charm and tranquil atmosphere. Stroll through the old town, visit the St. Vincent Cathedral, and soak in the serene ambiance. The cathedral, a national monument, showcases a blend of Romanesque and Gothic architecture.

St. Vincent Cathedral: Located at Place de la République, 07220 Viviers. Open daily from 9:00 AM to 6:00 PM. Entry is free.

Hidden Gems

1. Tain-l'Hermitage

Tain-l'Hermitage is a small town renowned for its vineyards and wine. A visit to the local vineyards offers a unique experience where you can taste world-class wines. Many vineyards provide guided tours and tastings for around $20 per person. Notable vineyards include Domaine Paul Jaboulet Aîné and Maison M. Chapoutier.

- Domaine Paul Jaboulet Aîné: Located at 25 Quai de la Liberté, 26600 Tain-l'Hermitage. Open Monday to Saturday from 10:00 AM to 6:00 PM. Tasting fee is $20.
- Maison M. Chapoutier: Located at 18 Avenue Dr Paul Durand, 26600 Tain-l'Hermitage. Open Monday to Saturday from 9:00 AM to 6:00 PM. Tasting fee is $20.

2. L'Isle-sur-la-Sorgue

Known as the "Venice of Provence," L'Isle-sur-la-Sorgue is famous for its antique shops and vibrant Sunday market. Wander through the charming streets, cross the picturesque canals, and explore the numerous antique stores. The market, held every Sunday, offers a wide variety of local produce, crafts, and antiques.

- L'Isle-sur-la-Sorgue Market: Held every Sunday from 7:00 AM to 2:00 PM. Located at the town center, 84800 L'Isle-sur-la-Sorgue.

3. Fondation Vincent van Gogh, Arles

For art lovers, the Fondation Vincent van Gogh in Arles offers a delightful experience. The museum houses a collection of works inspired by the artist, who spent a significant part of his life in the town. Entry is $10, and the museum often hosts temporary exhibitions showcasing contemporary art.

Fondation Vincent van Gogh: Located at 35 Rue Dr Fanton, 13200 Arles. Open Tuesday to Sunday from 11:00 AM to 6:00 PM. Entry fee is $10.

4. Montélimar

Montélimar is known for its nougat, a traditional French confection. Visit one of the local nougat factories, such as Nougat Arnaud Soubeyran, to see how this sweet treat is made. Factory tours are free, and you can sample various nougat flavors.

Nougat Arnaud Soubeyran: Located at 22 Avenue de Gournier, 26200 Montélimar. Open Monday to Saturday from 9:00 AM to 6:00 PM. Factory tours are free.

5. Perouges

Perouges, a medieval walled town, offers a step back in time with its cobblestone streets and well-preserved buildings. Take a guided tour to learn about the town's history and enjoy a slice of the local specialty, galette au sucre. Tours cost around $12 per person.

- Perouges Guided Tours: Start at the town center, 01800 Perouges. Open daily from 9:00 AM to 6:00 PM. Tour fee is $12.

6. Châteauneuf-du-Pape

This renowned wine region is a must-visit for wine enthusiasts. Take a guided tour of the vineyards and cellars, and enjoy tastings of some of the best wines in the world.

Tours typically cost around $30 to $50 per person and include multiple tastings. Notable wineries include Château Mont-Redon and Domaine de Beaurenard.

- Château Mont-Redon: Located at 84230 Châteauneuf-du-Pape. Open Monday to Saturday from 10:00 AM to 6:00 PM. Tasting fee is $30.
- Domaine de Beaurenard: Located at 10 Avenue Pierre de Luxembourg, 84230 Châteauneuf-du-Pape. Open Monday to Saturday from 10:00 AM to 6:00 PM. Tasting fee is $30.

7. Pont du Gard

The Pont du Gard, an ancient Roman aqueduct bridge, is a marvel of engineering and a UNESCO World Heritage site. A guided tour provides detailed information about its construction and history. Entry to the site is $10, with guided tours available for an additional fee.

Pont du Gard: Located at 400 Route du Pont du Gard, 30210 Vers-Pont-du-Gard. Open daily from 9:00 AM to 8:00 PM. Entry fee is $10.

8. Orange

Orange is home to the impressive Roman Theatre and Triumphal Arch, both UNESCO World Heritage sites. Guided tours of these ancient monuments offer insights into Roman architecture and history. The Roman Theatre, one of the best-preserved in Europe, hosts summer concerts and theatrical performances. Entry is around $9, and guided tours are available for an additional fee.

Roman Theatre: Located at Rue Madeleine Roch, 84100 Orange. Open daily from 9:00 AM to 6:00 PM. Entry fee is $9.

5.2 Outdoor Adventures: Cycling, Hiking, and Kayaking Along the Rhone

1. Cycling Along the Rhone

Cycling is one of the best ways to explore the Rhone Valley, offering an intimate and immersive experience of the region's natural beauty and cultural heritage. The ViaRhôna, a dedicated cycle route, stretches from Lake Geneva to the Mediterranean Sea, covering approximately 815 kilometers. This route passes through major cities, historic towns, and stunning countryside, making it an ideal choice for cyclists of all levels.

Popular Cycling Routes

- Lyon to Vienne: This 40-kilometer stretch is perfect for a day trip. Starting from Lyon, you'll cycle through urban landscapes before reaching the serene countryside. Vienne, with its rich Roman heritage, offers plenty of attractions such as the Roman Theatre and the Temple of Augustus and Livia. Bike rentals in Lyon cost around $20 to $30 per day, and guided tours are available for about $50 per person.
- Tain-l'Hermitage to Valence: This route takes you through the heart of wine country. Starting in Tain-l'Hermitage, famous for its vineyards, you can enjoy wine tastings before heading towards Valence. The path offers scenic views of the Rhone River and the surrounding countryside. Daily bike rentals are available for approximately $25, and guided tours cost around $60.
- Avignon to Arles: This 40-kilometer route offers a mix of history and natural beauty. Starting in Avignon, you'll cycle past the famous Pont d'Avignon and the

Palais des Papes before heading towards Arles, known for its Roman monuments and Van Gogh's legacy. Bike rentals are around $25 per day, with guided tours costing about $70 per person.

Tips for Cyclists

- Plan Your Route: Before setting off, plan your route and check the distance and difficulty level. Ensure you have a map or GPS device and know where you can stop for rest, food, and water.
- Safety Gear: Always wear a helmet and high-visibility clothing. Ensure your bike is in good condition, with working brakes and lights.
- Stay Hydrated: Carry enough water, especially during the summer months when temperatures can be high.
- Local Insights: Join a guided tour to benefit from local knowledge and insights. Guides can point out interesting landmarks and provide historical context.

2. Hiking Adventures

Hiking is another excellent way to explore the diverse landscapes of the Rhone Valley. The region offers numerous trails, ranging from easy walks to challenging hikes, each providing a unique perspective of the natural beauty and cultural heritage of the area.

Popular Hiking Trails

- Gorges de l'Ardèche: This area is known for its dramatic cliffs and stunning natural arches. The 30-kilometer trail through the Gorges de l'Ardèche offers breathtaking views and a chance to explore the Pont d'Arc, a natural stone arch over the river. Guided hikes cost around $50 per person and often include transportation and a picnic lunch.

- Dentelles de Montmirail: These rugged limestone peaks are a hiker's paradise. The trails wind through vineyards and forests, offering panoramic views of the Rhone Valley. The most popular trail is a 10-kilometer loop that takes about 4 hours to complete. Guided tours are available for approximately $40 per person.
- Camargue Regional Nature Park: This unique wetland area is home to diverse wildlife, including flamingos and wild horses. Hiking trails in the Camargue range from easy walks to more challenging routes. The Sentier des Méjeans is a 5-kilometer trail that takes about 2 hours to complete and offers excellent bird-watching opportunities. Guided hikes cost around $50 per person.

Tips for Hikers

- Proper Footwear: Wear sturdy hiking boots with good ankle support. The terrain can be uneven, especially on the more challenging trails.
- Weather Conditions: Check the weather forecast before heading out. Avoid hiking during extreme weather conditions, and always carry a rain jacket.
- Navigation: Bring a map and compass or a GPS device. Familiarize yourself with the trail markers and landmarks.
- Respect Nature: Stick to the marked trails to avoid damaging the environment. Carry out all trash and avoid disturbing wildlife.

3. Kayaking Along the Rhone

Kayaking offers a unique perspective of the Rhone River, allowing you to explore its tranquil waters and hidden coves. The river's calm sections are perfect for beginners, while more experienced kayakers can enjoy the thrill of navigating through gentle rapids.

Popular Kayaking Spots

- Ardèche Gorges: Known for its crystal-clear waters and stunning natural arches, the Ardèche Gorges is a popular kayaking destination. The 24-kilometer stretch from Vallon-Pont-d'Arc to Saint-Martin-d'Ardèche offers a mix of calm waters and exciting rapids. Guided tours, costing about $60 per person, include equipment, safety instructions, and a picnic.
- Sorgue River: Near Avignon, the Sorgue River is known for its clear waters and peaceful surroundings. The 8-kilometer stretch from Fontaine-de-Vaucluse to L'Isle-sur-la-Sorgue is perfect for a relaxing paddle. Kayak rentals cost around $30 per day, and guided tours are available for approximately $50.
- Camargue Wetlands: The Camargue's network of marshes and lagoons offers a unique kayaking experience. Paddle through narrow channels and open lagoons, observing the diverse wildlife. Guided tours, costing around $70 per person, provide insights into the region's ecology and history.

Tips for Kayakers

- Safety First: Always wear a life jacket and ensure your kayak is in good condition. Listen to the safety briefing and follow the guide's instructions.

- Paddling Technique: Use a steady, rhythmic stroke to conserve energy. Practice steering and maneuvering your kayak before setting off.
- Respect Wildlife: Maintain a safe distance from wildlife and avoid disturbing their habitats. The Rhone River is home to many protected species, so be mindful of your impact.

5.3 Cultural Immersion: Workshops, Demonstrations, and Local Interactions

Workshops

Cultural immersion is one of the most rewarding aspects of any travel experience, and the Rhone River Cruise offers numerous opportunities to engage deeply with the local traditions and crafts through a variety of workshops. These hands-on experiences not only provide insight into the regional culture but also allow you to create lasting memories and tangible souvenirs from your journey.

Cooking Classes in Lyon

Lyon, often regarded as the culinary capital of France, is an ideal place to take a cooking class and learn the secrets of French cuisine. These classes typically range from $80 to $120 per person and often include a market visit, hands-on cooking experience, and a delicious meal to enjoy at the end.

One highly recommended option is La Cuisine de Gagny (Address: 14 Rue des Capucins, 69001 Lyon, France). This renowned cooking school offers a variety of classes focusing on traditional Lyonnaise dishes. Imagine strolling through the bustling Lyon markets with a local chef, selecting fresh ingredients for your meal. The classes might include learning to prepare coq au vin, a classic French dish of chicken braised with wine, mushrooms, and onions, or mastering the art of tarte tatin, a delicious upside-down caramelized apple tart. The experience concludes with a communal meal where you can savor the fruits of your labor.

Perfume-Making in Avignon

In Avignon, you can delve into the world of fragrance at the Musée du Parfum (Address: 7 Rue des Teinturiers, 84000 Avignon, France). Perfume-making workshops here provide a unique opportunity to learn about the art of fragrance composition. For approximately $70, these workshops offer a comprehensive introduction to the history of perfume, the various scent families, and the techniques used to create a balanced fragrance.

During the workshop, you'll be guided by expert perfumers who will help you create your own signature scent. You'll leave with a personalized bottle of perfume, a perfect memento of your time in Avignon. These workshops are a fantastic way to engage with a traditional French craft and make for a luxurious and aromatic souvenir.

Painting Workshops in Arles

Arles, famous for its connection to Vincent van Gogh, is a haven for art enthusiasts. The Arles Art Workshop (Address: 12 Rue de la Liberté, 13200 Arles, France) offers painting workshops inspired by Van Gogh's masterpieces. These sessions, priced at about $50, include all materials and guidance from local artists.

Imagine setting up your easel in the same fields and streets that inspired Van Gogh. Under the guidance of a skilled artist, you can learn to capture the vibrant colors and unique light of the Provence region. Whether you're a seasoned painter or a beginner, these workshops offer a wonderful way to connect with the artistic heritage of Arles.

Wine Blending in Tain-l'Hermitage

Wine enthusiasts will find the wine blending workshops in Tain-l'Hermitage particularly fascinating. This town, renowned for its vineyards and wine production, offers hands-on experiences where you can learn about the intricacies of winemaking and create your own blend.

The Cité du Vin (Address: 1 Quai de la Cité, 26600 Tain-l'Hermitage, France) provides an excellent setting for these workshops. For around $90, participants can enjoy a guided tour of the vineyard, learn about the different grape varieties, and understand the aging process. The highlight is the blending session, where you can mix different wines to create a blend that suits your palate. You'll leave with a bottle of your own creation, a perfect keepsake from your visit.

Pottery Workshops in Viviers

Viviers, a small town known for its medieval charm, is also a center for pottery and ceramics. The Atelier de Poterie Viviers (Address: 6 Rue de la Cathedrale, 07220 Viviers, France) offers pottery workshops that allow you to work with clay and create your own pieces. These workshops typically cost around $40 to $60 and provide all the materials and instruction needed.

Participants can learn various techniques such as wheel throwing, hand building, and glazing. The workshop environment is both educational and relaxing, making it a perfect activity for those looking to engage in a creative endeavor. By the end of the session, you'll have your own handmade pottery to take home, a unique souvenir from your time in Viviers.

Cheese-Making in the Rhône Valley

The Rhône Valley is not only famous for its wines but also for its cheeses. Cheese-making workshops offer a delightful way to learn about this important aspect of French cuisine. One notable workshop is held at the Fromagerie de la Vallée (Address: 18 Route de Lyon, 26600 Mercurol-Veaunes, France).

For approximately $60, these workshops provide a comprehensive introduction to cheese-making. You'll learn about the different types of cheese, the milk sources, and the aging process. Participants get to make their own cheese, which can be taken home or enjoyed with a glass of local wine. This hands-on experience is both educational and delicious, offering a deeper appreciation for the region's culinary traditions.

Chocolate Workshops in Valence

For those with a sweet tooth, a chocolate workshop in Valence is a must. The Valrhona Cité du Chocolat (Address: 12 Avenue du Président Roosevelt, 26600 Tain-l'Hermitage, France) offers immersive workshops where you can learn about the art of chocolate making. These workshops, costing around $70, provide all the materials and guidance needed to create delicious chocolate treats.

Participants can learn to temper chocolate, create ganaches, and mold their own chocolate bars. The workshop includes tastings and a chance to take home your creations. It's a fantastic way to indulge in the rich, decadent flavors of French chocolate and understand the craftsmanship behind it.

Bread Baking in Lyon

Lyon's culinary scene isn't complete without its bakeries. The Lyon Baking Workshop (Address: 15 Rue des Archers, 69002 Lyon, France) offers bread baking classes that teach you the art of making traditional French bread. These workshops, priced at about $50, provide a hands-on experience in kneading, shaping, and baking bread.

Under the guidance of a master baker, you'll learn to make classic French baguettes, croissants, and other pastries. The aroma of freshly baked bread and the satisfaction of making your own loaves is an experience you won't forget. Participants get to take home their baked goods, a delicious reminder of their time in Lyon.

Silk Weaving in Lyon

Lyon has a rich history in silk weaving, and you can explore this heritage through silk weaving workshops. The Maison des Canuts (Address: 10 Rue d'Ivry, 69004 Lyon, France) offers workshops where you can learn about the silk-making process. For about $60, you'll get a tour of the museum and a hands-on session with a traditional loom.

Participants can try their hand at weaving and create a small piece of silk fabric to take home. This workshop provides a fascinating look into the craftsmanship and history of Lyon's silk industry, making it a unique and educational experience.

Glass Blowing in Arles

Glass blowing is another traditional craft you can explore during your Rhone River Cruise. The Arles Glass Workshop (Address: 22 Rue de la République, 13200 Arles, France) offers glass blowing workshops where you can learn to create your own glass art. These sessions, costing around $70, include all materials and instruction.

Under the guidance of experienced glassblowers, participants can learn to shape molten glass into beautiful pieces such as vases, ornaments, and jewelry. The workshop provides a unique opportunity to engage with an ancient craft and create something truly unique.

Textile Dyeing in Avignon

Textile dyeing workshops offer a colorful and creative way to engage with local crafts. The Avignon Textile Studio (Address: 5 Rue du Vieux Sextier, 84000 Avignon, France) offers workshops on natural dyeing techniques. For around $50, participants can learn to dye fabrics using natural ingredients such as plants, fruits, and vegetables.

These workshops provide an introduction to the history and techniques of textile dyeing. Participants can create their own dyed fabrics, which can be used to make scarves, garments, or home décor items. It's a vibrant and creative experience that allows you to explore the traditional art of dyeing.

Soap Making in Marseille

While not directly on the Rhone River, a day trip to Marseille offers the chance to learn about soap making, a craft with a long history in the region. The Savonnerie de la Licorne (Address: 34 Cours Julien, 13006 Marseille, France) offers soap making workshops where you can learn to make traditional Marseille soap. These workshops, costing around $40,provide all the materials and instruction needed to create your own bars of soap.

Participants can learn about the ingredients used in Marseille soap, such as olive oil and soda ash, and the traditional soap-making process. Under the guidance of expert soap makers, you'll get to mix, mold, and scent your soap, creating personalized bars to take home. It's a fun and educational experience that offers insight into the artisanal craftsmanship of Marseille soap.

CHAPTER SIX
MAKING THE MOST OF YOUR RHONE RIVER CRUISE

6.1 Packing Essentials: What to Bring for Comfort and Convenience

When embarking on a Rhone River cruise, packing wisely can make a significant difference in your comfort and overall experience. Here's a detailed guide on what to bring to ensure you're well-prepared for every aspect of your journey:

1. Clothing and Footwear:

- Layered Clothing: The weather along the Rhone can be unpredictable, with warm days and cool evenings. Bring a mix of short-sleeved shirts, long-sleeved shirts, sweaters, and a lightweight jacket. A waterproof windbreaker is essential for rainy days and windy conditions on the deck.
- Comfortable Footwear: You'll be doing a fair amount of walking during shore excursions. Comfortable walking shoes are a must. Pack a pair of dress shoes for formal dinners and events on the ship.
- Formal Attire: Most river cruises include at least one formal evening. Bring a nice dress or a suit and tie for these occasions.

2. Toiletries and Medications:

- Personal Toiletries: While most cruise ships provide basic toiletries, it's always a good idea to bring your preferred brands of shampoo, conditioner, body wash, and moisturizer. Don't forget your toothbrush, toothpaste, and any other personal hygiene products.

- Medications: Bring enough prescription medications to last the entire trip, plus a few extra days in case of delays. A small first-aid kit with band-aids, antiseptic cream, pain relievers, and motion sickness tablets can be very handy.
- Sunscreen and Insect Repellent: Protect your skin from the sun with a high-SPF sunscreen, and bring insect repellent for those warm evenings when mosquitoes might be present.

3. Electronics and Accessories:

- Camera and Accessories: Capture the stunning landscapes and charming towns along the Rhone with a good quality camera. Don't forget extra batteries, memory cards, and a charger. A lightweight tripod can help with low-light shots.
- Power Adapter: The standard voltage in France is 230V, and the plug types are C and E. Bring a universal power adapter to charge your devices.
- Portable Charger: A portable charger or power bank is essential for keeping your devices charged during long excursions.

4. Travel Documents and Essentials:

- Passport and Visas: Ensure your passport is valid for at least six months beyond your travel dates. Check if you need a visa for any of the countries you'll be visiting.
- Cruise Documents: Bring all necessary cruise documents, including your booking confirmation, itinerary, and any required health certificates or vaccination records.

- Money and Credit Cards: Carry some local currency for small purchases and tips. Major credit cards are widely accepted, but it's wise to inform your bank of your travel plans to avoid any issues.

5. Miscellaneous:

- Daypack: A small backpack or daypack is perfect for carrying essentials during shore excursions, such as a water bottle, snacks, a map, and your camera.
- Reusable Water Bottle: Staying hydrated is important. A reusable water bottle will help you avoid buying bottled water and reduce plastic waste.
- Travel Guide and Maps: A good travel guidebook and maps of the Rhone region can enhance your understanding and appreciation of the places you visit.
- By packing these essentials, you'll be well-prepared for a comfortable and enjoyable Rhone River cruise, ready to explore the picturesque landscapes and vibrant cultures along the way.

6.2 Photography Tips: Capturing the Beauty of the Rhone Valley

The Rhone Valley offers some of the most picturesque landscapes and charming towns in Europe, making it a paradise for photographers. Whether you're a seasoned photographer or a casual snap-happy traveler, these tips will help you capture stunning images of your journey:

1. Understanding Lighting:

- Golden Hours: The best times for photography are the golden hours, shortly after sunrise and before sunset. The soft, warm light during these periods creates

beautiful shadows and enhances the colors of the landscape.
- Midday Sun: While the light can be harsh around midday, you can still take great photos by seeking out shaded areas or using a polarizing filter to reduce glare and enhance the sky's color.

2. Composition Techniques:

- Rule of Thirds: Imagine your frame divided into nine equal parts by two horizontal and two vertical lines. Place your subject along these lines or at their intersections to create a balanced and engaging composition.
- Leading Lines: Use natural lines, such as roads, rivers, or pathways, to lead the viewer's eye into the photo and towards your main subject.
- Framing: Incorporate natural frames, like archways, trees, or windows, to draw attention to your subject and add depth to your photos.

3. Capturing Landscapes:

- Wide-Angle Lenses: Use a wide-angle lens to capture expansive landscapes and panoramic views. This lens allows you to include more of the scenery in your frame, creating a sense of vastness.
- Foreground Interest: Include elements in the foreground, such as flowers, rocks, or buildings, to add depth and context to your landscape shots.
- Reflections: Take advantage of reflections in the river, lakes, or puddles to create symmetrical compositions and add interest to your photos.

4. Photographing Towns and Architecture:

- Details and Close-Ups: Don't just focus on the big picture; look for interesting details like ornate door handles, colorful window shutters, or intricate architectural features.
- Street Photography: Capture the essence of the towns by photographing local markets, street performers, and everyday life. Be respectful and ask for permission if you're photographing people.
- Night Photography: Many towns along the Rhone are beautifully illuminated at night. Use a tripod to keep your camera steady and experiment with longer exposure times to capture the glow of streetlights and illuminated landmarks.

5. Wildlife and Nature Photography:

- Patience and Timing: Wildlife photography requires patience and good timing. Early mornings and late afternoons are often the best times to spot and photograph animals.
- Telephoto Lenses: A telephoto lens allows you to get close-up shots of wildlife without disturbing them. Use a fast shutter speed to freeze the action and avoid blurry images.
- Focus on Eyes: When photographing animals, make sure their eyes are in sharp focus. The eyes are the most expressive part of an animal and will draw the viewer's attention.

6. Post-Processing Tips:

- Editing Software: Use photo editing software like Adobe Lightroom or Photoshop to enhance your images. Adjust the exposure, contrast, and colors to bring out the best in your photos.

- Cropping and Straightening: Crop your images to improve composition and remove any distracting elements. Straighten your photos to ensure horizons and buildings are level.
- Sharpening and Noise Reduction: Apply sharpening to enhance the details in your photos and use noise reduction to minimize graininess, especially in low-light images.

By following these photography tips, you'll be able to capture the stunning beauty of the Rhone Valley and create lasting memories of your river cruise. Whether you're photographing landscapes, architecture, wildlife, or local life, each image will tell a unique story of your journey.

6.3 Staying Connected: Internet Access and Communication Options

Staying connected while cruising the Rhone River is important for many travelers, whether for keeping in touch with loved ones, sharing your travel experiences on social media, or handling work-related tasks. Here's a comprehensive guide on how to stay connected during your cruise:

1. Onboard Internet Access:

- Wi-Fi Availability: Most river cruise ships offer Wi-Fi access throughout the vessel, including cabins, common areas, and dining rooms. However, the speed and reliability of the connection can vary depending on the ship and its location on the river.
- Internet Packages: Cruise lines typically offer various internet packages, ranging from basic email and browsing plans to more expensive packages that support streaming and large downloads. Prices can

range from $10 to $50 per day, depending on the level of service.

- Usage Tips: To make the most of your onboard internet access, use Wi-Fi during off-peak hours (early morning or late evening) when fewer passengers are online. Download any large files, movies, or music before your trip to minimize bandwidth usage.

2. Local SIM Cards and Mobile Data:

- Buying a Local SIM Card: If you prefer to use your smartphone for internet access, consider purchasing a local SIM card upon arrival in France. Major providers like Orange, SFR, and Bouygues Telecom offer prepaid SIM cards with data plans starting at around $20 for 5GB of data.
- Activation and Compatibility: Ensure your phone is unlocked and compatible with European networks. Activation is usually straightforward, and you can find SIM cards at airports, convenience stores, and mobile phone shops.
- Data Roaming: Check with your mobile carrier about international roaming plans. Some carriers offer affordable daily or weekly data packages for use in Europe, which can be convenient if you don't want to switch SIM cards.

3. Staying Connected in Ports:

- Free Wi-Fi in Towns: Many towns along the Rhone River offer free Wi-Fi in public areas, such as town squares, cafes, and tourist information centers. Look for Wi-Fi signs or ask locals for the nearest hotspot.
- Cafes and Restaurants: Enjoy a coffee or meal at a local cafe or restaurant that offers free Wi-Fi. This is a

great way to stay connected while experiencing the local culture and cuisine.

- Public Libraries and Tourist Centers: Public libraries and tourist information centers often provide free internet access and computer terminals for visitors. These can be handyresources for checking emails, researching attractions, or making travel arrangements.

4. Communication Apps:

- Voice and Video Calls: Use apps like Skype, WhatsApp, or FaceTime to make voice and video calls over Wi-Fi or mobile data. This is a convenient and cost-effective way to stay in touch with friends and family back home.
- Messaging Apps: Stay connected with instant messaging apps like WhatsApp, Facebook Messenger, or Telegram. These apps allow you to send text messages, photos, and videos to individuals or groups without using cellular minutes or SMS.
- Social Media Platforms: Share your travel experiences in real-time on social media platforms like Instagram, Facebook, or Twitter. Post photos, videos, and updates about your Rhone River cruise to keep your followers engaged and informed.

5. Emergency Communication:

- Emergency Contacts: Keep a list of emergency contacts handy, including the cruise ship's contact information, local emergency services, and the nearest embassy or consulate.
- Medical Assistance: If you require medical assistance while on board or in port, notify the ship's crew or

seek help from local medical facilities. Most cruise ships have onboard medical staff and facilities to handle minor injuries and illnesses.

- Travel Insurance: Consider purchasing travel insurance that includes coverage for medical emergencies, trip interruptions, and lost or stolen belongings. This provides peace of mind and financial protection in case of unexpected incidents.

By utilizing these communication options, you can stay connected and informed throughout your Rhone River cruise, whether you're sharing your adventures with loved ones, accessing essential information, or seeking assistance in case of emergencies.

CHAPTER SEVEN
BEYOND THE CRUISE: EXTENDED STAY OPTIONS

7.1 Marseille: Gateway to the Mediterranean

Marseille, the vibrant port city of the Mediterranean, offers a captivating blend of history, culture, and seaside charm. As you step off your Rhone River cruise, extend your journey with an exploration of Marseille and its surrounding treasures.

7.1.1 Discovering Marseille's Maritime History: Vieux Port, Château d'If

Marseille, the sun-drenched jewel of the Mediterranean, is a city steeped in history and brimming with vibrant culture. As the second-largest city in France and the oldest, founded around 600 BC by Greek sailors from Phocaea, Marseille has long been a melting pot of cultures and traditions. This diverse heritage is palpable in every corner, from the bustling Vieux Port to the serene coastal escapes. For travelers extending their Rhone River cruise, Marseille offers a wealth of experiences that promise to captivate and enchant.

Discovering Marseille's Maritime History: Vieux Port and Château d'If

1. Vieux Port

The Vieux Port, or Old Port, is the beating heart of Marseille. This historic harbor has been a focal point of the city for over 2,600 years, serving as a gateway for trade and cultural exchange. Today, it remains a lively hub where the city's maritime spirit is on full display.

Exploration Tips: Begin your day with a stroll along the quays, where you'll find a vibrant mix of fishermen selling their catch, pleasure boats, and luxury yachts. The morning fish market is a must-see, offering a glimpse into the daily life of the locals and a chance to sample the freshest seafood.

Activities: Take a leisurely boat tour of the harbor for a different perspective of the city and to appreciate its stunning waterfront. Numerous operators offer guided tours, with prices averaging around $15 to $25 USD per person. For a more immersive experience, consider renting a small boat for a couple of hours.

Dining: The area around Vieux Port is packed with excellent restaurants and cafes. Enjoy a meal at La Brasserie du Port, where you can savor traditional Bouillabaisse, Marseille's famous fish stew. Expect to pay around $30 to $50 USD for a meal.

Accommodation: Stay at the Radisson Blu Hotel Marseille Vieux Port, offering stunning views of the harbor. Room rates start at approximately $200 USD per night. Address: 38-40 Quai de Rive Neuve, 13007 Marseille, France.

2. Château d'If

A short boat ride from the Vieux Port lies the Château d'If, a fortress steeped in legend and history. Built in the 16th century on the orders of King Francis I, it was initially intended to defend against naval attacks but soon became infamous as a prison.

Historical Significance: The Château d'If is best known as the setting for Alexandre Dumas' classic novel "The Count of Monte Cristo." Visitors can explore the dungeons and cells where prisoners were once held, including the supposed cell of Edmond Dantès, the novel's protagonist.

Visiting Tips: Boats to the Château d'If depart regularly from the Vieux Port, with round-trip tickets costing about $8 to $10 USD. It's advisable to check the schedule and book in advance, especially during peak tourist season. Opening hours are typically from 9:00 AM to 6:00 PM, but it's best to verify current timings.

Experience: The island offers breathtaking views of the Marseille coastline and the Mediterranean Sea. Bring comfortable walking shoes and a camera to capture the stunning scenery.

7.1.2 Coastal Escapes: Cassis, Calanques National Park, and the Blue Coast

As you continue your journey beyond the Rhone River cruise, the coastal escapes of Cassis, Calanques National Park, and the Blue Coast offer a breathtaking contrast to the riverine landscapes. Nestled along the stunning Mediterranean coast, these destinations promise an enchanting blend of natural beauty, adventure, and relaxation. Here's an in-depth guide to making the most of your time in these captivating locales.

Cassis: A Mediterranean Gem

Exploring the Town of Cassis

Cassis, a picturesque fishing village turned chic seaside resort, exudes charm and tranquility. The town's narrow streets are lined with pastel-colored houses, boutique shops, and bustling cafes, inviting you to wander and soak in the ambiance. Start your exploration at the port, where traditional fishing boats and luxurious yachts bob in the clear blue waters.

A must-visit spot in Cassis is the Place Baragnon, a lively square surrounded by shops and eateries. Enjoy a leisurely coffee at one of the outdoor cafes and watch the world go by. For those interested in local history, the Cassis Museum (Rue Xavier d'Authier, 13260 Cassis) offers insights into the town's maritime heritage and wine-making traditions. Admission is free, and the museum is open daily from 10:00 AM to 6:00 PM.

Cassis Market: A Feast for the Senses

No visit to Cassis is complete without a trip to its vibrant market, held every Wednesday and Friday morning at Place Baragnon. Here, you'll find an array of fresh produce, artisanal cheeses, cured meats, and locally made crafts. The market is a sensory delight, with the aromas of fresh herbs and spices mingling with the scent of the sea. Take the opportunity to purchase some local specialties, such as olive oil, lavender products, or a bottle of Cassis wine.

Dining in Cassis

Cassis boasts a variety of dining options, from casual beachside eateries to gourmet restaurants. For an unforgettable meal, head to La Villa Madie (Avenue de Revestel, Anse de Corton, 13260 Cassis), a Michelin-starred restaurant known for its exquisite Mediterranean cuisine and stunning sea views. Expect to spend around $100 to $200 USD per person for a multi-course tasting menu. The restaurant is open for lunch and dinner from Wednesday to Sunday.

For a more casual dining experience, try Chez Gilbert (19 Quai des Baux, 13260 Cassis), a popular seafood restaurant located right on the harbor. Savor fresh oysters, bouillabaisse, and other local seafood dishes while enjoying views of the picturesque port. Prices range from $30 to $70

USD per person. Chez Gilbert is open daily for lunch and dinner.

Calanques National Park: Nature's Masterpiece

Discovering the Calanques

The Calanques National Park, stretching between Marseille and Cassis, is a natural wonderland of towering limestone cliffs, hidden coves, and crystal-clear waters. This protected area is renowned for its dramatic landscapes and biodiversity, making it a haven for outdoor enthusiasts.

Hiking in the Calanques

Hiking is one of the best ways to explore the Calanques. Several well-marked trails offer varying levels of difficulty, from leisurely walks to challenging treks. One of the most popular routes is the hike from Cassis to Calanque d'En-Vau, which takes approximately three to four hours round trip. The trail winds through rugged terrain, offering spectacular views of the cliffs and Mediterranean Sea. Be sure to wear sturdy hiking shoes and bring plenty of water, as there are no facilities along the trail.

For those seeking a guided experience, several local companies offer hiking tours of the Calanques. Prices typically range from $50 to $100 USD per person, depending on the duration and level of difficulty of the hike.

Boat Tours: Exploring by Sea

Another fantastic way to experience the Calanques is by boat. Numerous operators in Cassis offer boat tours ranging from one-hour excursions to full-day adventures. These tours provide a unique perspective of the Calanques, allowing you to explore hidden coves and sea caves that are inaccessible by land.

One highly recommended option is the three-hour boat tour, which includes stops at several of the most beautiful calanques, such as Calanque de Port-Miou, Calanque de Port-Pin, and Calanque d'En-Vau. Prices for boat tours vary, but you can expect to pay around $40 to $60 USD per person. Most tours operate daily from April to October, with multiple departures throughout the day.

The Blue Coast: Scenic Beauty and Hidden Treasures

Scenic Drives Along the Blue Coast

The Blue Coast, or Côte Bleue, is a stunning stretch of coastline between Marseille and Martigues, known for its picturesque villages, secluded beaches, and dramatic cliffs. One of the best ways to explore this region is by car, taking a scenic drive along the Route de la Côte Bleue.

As you drive, you'll encounter breathtaking viewpoints, charming fishing villages, and inviting beaches. Be sure to stop at the village of Carry-le-Rouet, often referred to as the "Pearl of the Blue Coast." This quaint town offers beautiful beaches, a bustling marina, and a variety of seafood restaurants. For a delicious meal with a view, try La Crique (Chemin de la Plage de la Crique, 13620 Carry-le-Rouet), where you can enjoy fresh seafood dishes while overlooking the Mediterranean. Prices range from $30 to $60 USD per person.

Beaches of the Blue Coast

The Blue Coast is home to some of the most beautiful beaches in the region, perfect for swimming, sunbathing, and snorkeling. Plage du Rouet in Carry-le-Rouet is a popular spot with clear waters and sandy shores, ideal for families and water sports enthusiasts. The beach is equipped with showers, restrooms, and several beachside cafes.

For a more secluded experience, visit the hidden gem of Plage de la Saulce in Sausset-les-Pins. This small, pebbly beach is surrounded by rocky cliffs and offers a peaceful escape from the crowds. Pack a picnic and spend the day relaxing by the water, or explore the nearby rock pools teeming with marine life.

Outdoor Activities on the Blue Coast

The Blue Coast offers a wealth of outdoor activities for nature lovers and adventure seekers. In addition to hiking and beach activities, the region is known for its excellent scuba diving and snorkeling opportunities. The underwater landscapes are rich with marine life, including colorful fish, sea anemones, and even the occasional octopus.

Several dive centers in Carry-le-Rouet and Sausset-les-Pins offer guided dives and snorkeling excursions, catering to all skill levels. Prices for a guided dive typically range from $60 to $120 USD per person, including equipment rental. For snorkeling, expect to pay around $30 to $50 USD per person.

Tips for Making the Most of Your Coastal Escapes

1. Best Time to Visit

The best time to visit Cassis, Calanques National Park, and the Blue Coast is during the spring (April to June) and fall (September to October) when the weather is pleasant, and the crowds are smaller. Summer (July to August) can be quite busy, with higher temperatures and more tourists, but it's also the perfect time for enjoying the beaches and outdoor activities.

2. Getting Around

While Cassis is easily walkable, having a car is highly recommended for exploring the Calanques and Blue Coast. Car rentals are available in Cassis and Marseille, with prices starting at around $40 USD per day. Public transportation is limited in this region, so having your own vehicle provides the flexibility to explore at your own pace.

3. What to Bring

When visiting these coastal escapes, be sure to pack essentials such as sunscreen, a hat, sunglasses, and plenty of water. Comfortable walking shoes are a must for exploring the Calanques, and a swimsuit is essential for enjoying the beaches. If you plan to hike or take a boat tour, bring a light jacket or windbreaker, as it can get breezy near the coast.

4. Respecting Nature

The natural beauty of Cassis, Calanques National Park, and the Blue Coast is a precious resource that must be preserved. When exploring these areas, follow the principles of Leave No Trace: take only pictures, leave only footprints. Dispose of waste properly, stay on marked trails, and avoid disturbing wildlife. By respecting the environment, you help ensure that these coastal escapes remain pristine for future generations to enjoy.

Cassis, Calanques National Park, and the Blue Coast offer an unforgettable blend of natural beauty, cultural richness, and outdoor adventure.

7.2 Paris: The City of Light

Paris, the epitome of romance and sophistication, beckons with its timeless landmarks, world-class art, and culinary delights. Extend your Rhone River cruise with a sojourn in the City of Light, where every street corner reveals a new treasure waiting to be discovered.

7.2.1 Iconic Landmarks: Eiffel Tower, Louvre Museum, Notre-Dame Cathedral

1. Eiffel Tower: A Symbol of Paris

The Eiffel Tower, standing tall at 324 meters, is an iconic symbol of Paris and a must-visit for anyone extending their Rhone River cruise to the City of Light. Constructed by Gustave Eiffel for the 1889 World's Fair, this architectural marvel attracts millions of visitors each year.

Visiting the Eiffel Tower

Begin your visit by taking an elevator ride to the top for breathtaking panoramic views of Paris. The tower has three levels accessible to the public:

- First Level: At 57 meters, the first level offers a glass floor, an immersive experience about the tower's history, and the 58 Tour Eiffel restaurant, where you can enjoy a meal with a view.
- Second Level: At 115 meters, this level provides an excellent vantage point for viewing landmarks such as the Arc de Triomphe and the Seine River. It also hosts the Jules Verne restaurant, known for its gourmet French cuisine.
- Summit: At 276 meters, the summit is accessible via a second elevator from the second level. Here, you can

visit Gustave Eiffel's office and enjoy a glass of champagne at the Champagne Bar.

Tips for Visiting

- Tickets: Purchase tickets online in advance to avoid long queues. Prices start at approximately $20 USD for adults, with discounts for children and youths.
- Best Time to Visit: Early morning or late evening visits are ideal to avoid crowds. The tower is open daily from 9:30 AM to 11:45 PM, extending to midnight during the summer months.
- Accessibility: The tower is accessible to visitors with disabilities, with elevators available to the first and second levels.

Nearby Attractions

After your visit, explore the nearby Trocadéro Gardens, where you can capture stunning photos of the Eiffel Tower, or take a leisurely boat ride along the Seine for a different perspective.

2. Louvre Museum: A Treasure Trove of Art

The Louvre Museum, housed in the former royal palace, is the world's largest art museum and a historic monument in Paris. With over 35,000 artworks on display, it is home to some of the most famous masterpieces, including the Mona Lisa and the Venus de Milo.

Exploring the Louvre

1. Entrance and Highlights:

- Pyramide Entrance: The main entrance is through the glass pyramid in the courtyard. Alternatively, use the Carrousel du Louvre entrance for quicker access.
- Denon Wing: This wing houses the Mona Lisa, Winged Victory of Samothrace, and other Italian Renaissance masterpieces.
- Sully Wing: Here, you'll find the medieval foundations of the Louvre and the famed Venus de Milo.
- Richelieu Wing: Home to the apartments of Napoleon III, the Code of Hammurabi, and extensive collections of decorative arts.

2. Visitor Tips

- Tickets: Purchase tickets online for approximately $18 USD. Admission is free for visitors under 18 and for EU residents under 26.
- Audio Guides: Available in multiple languages, audio guides enhance your visit with detailed information about the artworks.
- Tours: Consider joining a guided tour to gain deeper insights into the museum's vast collection.
- Best Time to Visit: Arrive early or visit on Wednesday and Friday evenings when the museum is open until 9:45 PM. The museum is closed on Tuesdays.

3. Amenities and Services

- Dining: Several cafes and restaurants are available, including Café Marly, overlooking the pyramid, and the chic Bistrot Benoit.
- Shops: The museum's boutiques offer a range of art books, replicas, and souvenirs.

Nearby Attractions

Tuileries Garden: Adjacent to the Louvre, this public garden is perfect for a relaxing stroll or picnic.

Orsay Museum: A short walk away, the Orsay Museum features an extensive collection of Impressionist and post-Impressionist masterpieces.

3. Notre-Dame Cathedral: Gothic Splendor

Notre-Dame Cathedral, with its iconic twin towers and intricate facade, is a masterpiece of French Gothic architecture. Although it is currently undergoing restoration after the 2019 fire, it remains a must-see landmark.

Exploring Notre-Dame

1. Exterior and Surroundings:

- Facade: Admire the west facade, featuring the Gallery of Kings, rose windows, and detailed sculptures.
- Towers: The twin towers offer panoramic views of Paris, accessible via a 387-step climb. Although currently closed for restoration, keep an eye on reopening dates.
- Parvis: The square in front of the cathedral provides a great vantage point for photographs.

2. Interior Highlights:

- Nave: The soaring nave, with its ribbed vaults and stained glass windows, creates an awe-inspiring atmosphere.
- Rose Windows: The north and south rose windows are masterpieces of medieval stained glass, depicting biblical scenes.
- Chapels: Explore the side chapels, each dedicated to different saints and adorned with beautiful artworks.

- Crypt: The crypt beneath the cathedral houses archaeological remains from Roman times to the Middle Ages.

3. Visiting Tips

- Admission: Entrance to the cathedral is free, but donations are encouraged to support the restoration efforts.
- Best Time to Visit: Early morning or late afternoon to avoid peak tourist hours.
- Dress Code: Modest attire is required, as Notre-Dame is an active place of worship.
- Masses and Services: Attend a mass or vespers for a unique spiritual experience. Check the cathedral's website for schedules.

Nearby Attractions

Île de la Cité: Wander around the historic island, home to Sainte-Chapelle, with its stunning stained glass, and the Conciergerie, a former royal palace and prison.

Shakespeare and Company: This famous English-language bookstore, located nearby, is a haven for book lovers and a literary landmark.

Making the Most of Your Visit

1. Eiffel Tower

To truly appreciate the Eiffel Tower, consider visiting during different times of the day. Early morning visits offer a serene atmosphere and fewer crowds, while evening visits allow you to witness the tower illuminated against the night sky. The tower sparkles for five minutes every hour after dusk, providing a magical experience.

2. Louvre Museum

With its vast collection, it's impossible to see everything in one visit. Prioritize the highlights, but also leave time to wander and discover lesser-known treasures. The Louvre's layout can be overwhelming, so download a map from the museum's website or use the Louvre's app for navigation.

3. Notre-Dame Cathedral

Even during restoration, the area around Notre-Dame offers plenty to explore. Take a Seine River cruise for a unique view of the cathedral and other landmarks. Evening cruises often include dinner and provide a romantic setting to see Paris illuminated.

Practical Information

1. Eiffel Tower:

Address: Champ de Mars, 5 Avenue Anatole France, 75007 Paris, France

2. Louvre Museum:

Address: Rue de Rivoli, 75001 Paris, France

3. Notre-Dame Cathedral:

Address: 6 Parvis Notre-Dame – Pl. Jean-Paul II, 75004 Paris, France

7.2.2 Cultural Immersion: Theater, Opera, and Fashion

Theater in Paris

Paris boasts a vibrant theater scene, with a rich history that spans centuries. The city's theaters offer a diverse array of performances, from classical plays to modern dramas, ensuring there's something for everyone.

1. Palais Garnier

The Palais Garnier, also known as the Opéra Garnier, is one of Paris's most famous landmarks. This opulent opera house, with its grand staircase, gilded interiors, and stunning chandeliers, is a masterpiece of 19th-century architecture. It's not just a place to watch a performance; it's an experience in itself.

What to See

At the Palais Garnier, you can enjoy a variety of performances, including opera, ballet, and classical concerts. The Paris Opera Ballet, one of the most prestigious ballet companies in the world, frequently performs here. Tickets can be purchased online or at the box office, with prices ranging from $50 to $300 USD, depending on the performance and seating.

Insider Tips

To enhance your experience, consider taking a guided tour of the Palais Garnier. These tours offer a behind-the-scenes look at the opera house, including access to areas not typically open to the public. Tours are available daily, with tickets priced at approximately $20 USD.

2. Théâtre de la Ville

For those interested in contemporary theater, the Théâtre de la Ville is a must-visit. Located in the heart of Paris, this theater is known for its innovative productions and diverse programming, which includes dance, music, and theater from around the world.

What to See

The Théâtre de la Ville hosts a wide range of performances, from avant-garde theater to international dance troupes. Check their website for the latest schedule and ticket information. Prices generally range from $20 to $100 USD, making it an affordable cultural outing.

Insider Tips

To get the most out of your visit, consider joining the Théâtre de la Ville's membership program. Members receive discounts on tickets, priority booking, and invitations to special events. Membership fees vary but typically start at around $50 USD per year.

3. La Comédie-Française

Founded in 1680, La Comédie-Française is one of the oldest active theaters in the world. It specializes in French classical theater, with a repertoire that includes works by Molière, Racine, and Corneille. The theater's elegant interior and historic ambiance provide a perfect setting for these timeless plays.

What to See

La Comédie-Française offers performances year-round, with a schedule that includes both classic and contemporary works. Ticket prices range from $30 to $150 USD, depending on the performance and seating. Performances are primarily in French, but some productions offer English subtitles or audio guides.

Insider Tips

If you're a student or under 28, take advantage of the theater's youth pricing, which offers significant discounts on tickets. Additionally, same-day tickets for unsold seats are often available at reduced prices.

Opera in Paris

Paris is home to some of the world's most prestigious opera houses, where you can experience the magic of opera and ballet in breathtaking settings.

1. Opéra Bastille

The modern counterpart to the Palais Garnier, the Opéra Bastille is a state-of-the-art opera house that hosts performances by the Paris Opera. Located in the bustling Bastille district, this venue combines cutting-edge design with world-class acoustics.

What to See

The Opéra Bastille's repertoire includes opera, ballet, and orchestral concerts. Performances range from classic operas by composers like Verdi and Wagner to contemporary works. Tickets can be purchased online or at the box office, with prices ranging from $20 to $200 USD.

Insider Tips

For a more intimate experience, consider attending one of the Opéra Bastille's lunchtime concerts. These shorter performances offer a taste of the opera house's repertoire at a fraction of the cost. Lunchtime concert tickets are typically priced around $10 to $30 USD.

2. Théâtre des Champs-Élysées

Located on the famous Avenue Montaigne, the Théâtre des Champs-Élysées is a renowned venue for opera, ballet, and classical music. The theater's Art Deco architecture and elegant interior create a sophisticated ambiance for its high-quality performances.

What to See

The Théâtre des Champs-Élysées hosts a variety of performances, including operas, ballets, and symphony concerts. The theater is particularly known for its excellent acoustics and the quality of its productions. Ticket prices range from $30 to $150 USD.

Insider Tips

Check the theater's website for special offers and subscription packages, which can provide significant savings if you plan to attend multiple performances. Additionally, the theater often hosts free pre-performance talks and lectures that provide valuable insights into the evening's program.

Fashion in Paris

Paris is the fashion capital of the world, and no visit to the city would be complete without exploring its vibrant fashion scene. From haute couture boutiques to vintage shops, Paris offers a wealth of opportunities for fashion enthusiasts.

1. Avenue des Champs-Élysées

The Avenue des Champs-Élysées is one of the most famous shopping streets in the world. Here, you'll find flagship stores for luxury brands like Louis Vuitton, Cartier, and Chanel, as well as high-street favorites like Zara and H&M.

What to Buy

While strolling along the Champs-Élysées, be sure to stop by the Louis Vuitton flagship store. This multi-story boutique offers an extensive selection of the brand's iconic handbags, luggage, and accessories. Prices for Louis Vuitton items start at around $200 USD for smaller accessories and can reach several thousand dollars for larger items.

Insider Tips

For a truly unique shopping experience, visit the Champs-Élysées in the evening when the street is beautifully illuminated. Many stores stay open late, allowing you to enjoy a leisurely shopping experience after a day of sightseeing.

2. Le Marais

The Marais district is known for its eclectic mix of trendy boutiques, vintage shops, and independent designers. This fashionable neighborhood is the perfect place to discover one-of-a-kind pieces and support local artisans.

What to Buy

Le Marais is home to numerous vintage shops, where you can find everything from retro clothing to antique jewelry. One of the most popular shops is Kilo Shop (69-71 Rue de la Verrerie, 75004 Paris), which sells vintage clothing by weight. Prices vary, but you can expect to pay around $20 to $50 USD for most items.

Insider Tips

Visit Le Marais on a Sunday, when many of the district's shops are open, unlike in other parts of Paris. This is also the perfect time to explore the neighborhood's lively street markets and food stalls.

3. Galeries Lafayette

For a luxurious shopping experience, head to Galeries Lafayette, one of Paris's premier department stores. Located near the Opéra Garnier, this iconic store offers a wide range of high-end fashion, beauty products, and gourmet food.

What to Buy

Galeries Lafayette is the place to splurge on designer clothing, shoes, and accessories. The store features an impressive selection of French and international brands, including Chanel, Dior, and Gucci. Prices vary widely, with luxury items typically starting at around $200 USD.

Insider Tips

Don't miss the store's stunning rooftop terrace, which offers panoramic views of Paris. The terrace is free to access and provides a perfect spot for taking photos or enjoying a coffee from the rooftop café.

Exploring Parisian Fashion Houses

For a deeper dive into Paris's fashion scene, consider visiting some of the city's renowned fashion houses. Many offer guided tours, workshops, and even bespoke shopping experiences.

1. Christian Dior Museum

Located in the chic 8th arrondissement, the Christian Dior Museum offers an intimate look at the life and work of one of fashion's most legendary designers. The museum features rotating exhibitions that showcase Dior's iconic designs and the history of the house.

What to See

Exhibitions at the Christian Dior Museum often include rare archival pieces, sketches, and personal artifacts from Dior's life. Admission prices typically range from $15 to $25 USD. Check the museum's website for current exhibition details and opening hours.

Insider Tips

Book your tickets in advance, as the museum can get quite busy, especially during special exhibitions. Consider visiting during the week to avoid the weekend crowds.

2. Yves Saint Laurent Museum

Another must-visit for fashion enthusiasts is the Yves Saint Laurent Museum. Located in the former couture house of Yves Saint Laurent, the museum offers a comprehensive look at the designer's career and his most iconic creations.

What to See

The museum's permanent collection includes some of Saint Laurent's most famous designs, as well as sketches, photographs, and personal items. Admission is approximately $15 to $20 USD. Opening hours are generally from 11:00 AM to 6:00 PM, closed on Mondays.

Insider Tips

Join a guided tour to gain deeper insights into Saint Laurent's creative process and the history of the fashion house. Tours are available in multiple languages and can be booked through the museum's website.

3. Attending Paris Fashion Week

If you're a true fashion aficionado, consider timing your visit to coincide with Paris Fashion Week. Held twice a year, in February/March and September/October, Paris Fashion Week is one of the most important events in the fashion calendar.

What to See

ParisFashion Week showcases the latest collections from top designers and brands, attracting fashion insiders, celebrities, and influencers from around the world. While tickets to runway shows are typically reserved for industry professionals, there are still plenty of opportunities to experience the excitement of Fashion Week.

Insider Tips

Keep an eye out for Fashion Week-related events and parties, which often take place at venues across the city. These events may include pop-up shops, fashion exhibitions, and celebrity sightings. Follow fashion influencers and bloggers on social media for insider tips and recommendations on where to go.

7.2.3 Culinary Delights: Michelin-Starred Restaurants, Patisseries, and Markets

Michelin-Starred Restaurants

Paris is home to some of the world's finest Michelin-starred restaurants, where culinary artistry and exceptional service come together to create unforgettable dining experiences. Here are a few must-visit establishments:

1. Le Bernardin

- Address: 7-9 Rue de la Paix, 75002 Paris, France
- Average Cost: $250 - $500 per person
- Opening Hours: Monday to Friday, 12:00 PM - 2:30 PM, 7:00 PM - 10:30 PM

Le Bernardin, a three-Michelin-starred restaurant, is synonymous with seafood excellence. Helmed by Chef Éric Ripert, the restaurant offers a menu that celebrates the freshest catches from the sea. Signature dishes include the Thinly Pounded Yellowfin Tuna and the Lobster in a Spiced Red Wine Sauce. Reservations are essential, and the tasting menu, priced at around $350 per person, promises an exquisite culinary adventure.

2. Alain Ducasse au Plaza Athénée

- Address: 25 Avenue Montaigne, 75008 Paris, France
- Average Cost: $200 - $450 per person
- Opening Hours: Monday to Friday, 12:30 PM - 2:15 PM, 7:30 PM - 10:00 PM

This iconic three-Michelin-starred restaurant, located within the luxurious Plaza Athénée Hotel, offers a dining experience that emphasizes naturalness and simplicity. Chef Alain Ducasse's innovative approach focuses on the trilogy of fish, vegetables, and cereals. The restaurant's opulent setting and dishes like the Blue Lobster with Seaweed Butter and the Chilled Tomato Water with Gold Leaf make for a memorable dining experience. The tasting menu starts at approximately $320 per person.

3. Guy Savoy

- Address: Monnaie de Paris, 11 Quai de Conti, 75006 Paris, France

- Average Cost: $300 - $500 per person
- Opening Hours: Tuesday to Friday, 12:00 PM - 2:30 PM, 7:00 PM - 10:30 PM

Guy Savoy's eponymous restaurant, located in the historic Monnaie de Paris, offers a gastronomic journey through modern French cuisine. With three Michelin stars, the restaurant is renowned for its elegant dishes and impeccable service. Highlights include the Artichoke and Black Truffle Soup and the Lobster with Coral Sauce. The tasting menu, priced at around $380 per person, showcases the chef's creative mastery.

Patisseries

Parisian patisseries are a paradise for those with a sweet tooth. From flaky croissants to delicate macarons, the city's patisseries offer an array of delectable treats. Here are some top spots to indulge in Parisian pastries:

1. Ladurée

- Address: 75 Avenue des Champs-Élysées, 75008 Paris, France
- Average Cost: $2 - $5 per macaron
- Opening Hours: Monday to Sunday, 7:30 AM - 11:00 PM

Ladurée is an iconic Parisian patisserie famed for its macarons. Founded in 1862, Ladurée's elegant salons de thé (tea rooms) are perfect for enjoying a leisurely afternoon tea. The patisserie's macarons, available in a variety of flavors such as rose, pistachio, and salted caramel, are a must-try. A box of six macarons costs around $18, making it a delightful souvenir to take home.

2. Pierre Hermé

- Address: 72 Rue Bonaparte, 75006 Paris, France
- Average Cost: $2 - $6 per pastry
- Opening Hours: Monday to Sunday, 10:00 AM - 7:00 PM

Pierre Hermé, often referred to as the Picasso of Pastry, offers innovative and exquisite pastries that push the boundaries of traditional patisserie. Signature creations include the Ispahan, a macaron filled with rose, lychee, and raspberry, and the Mogador, a passion fruit and milk chocolate combination. The seasonal collections and unique flavor combinations make Pierre Hermé a must-visit for pastry enthusiasts.

3. La Maison du Chocolat

- Address: 225 Rue du Faubourg Saint-Honoré, 75008 Paris, France
- Average Cost: $10 - $50 per box
- Opening Hours: Monday to Saturday, 10:00 AM - 7:00 PM

For chocolate lovers, La Maison du Chocolat is a dream come true. Founded in 1977 by Robert Linxe, this patisserie specializes in handcrafted chocolates and decadent pastries. The Éclair au Chocolat and the Truffle Palet are standout treats. A visit to La Maison du Chocolat offers a chance to indulge in luxurious chocolates and learn about the art of chocolate making.

Markets

Parisian markets are vibrant hubs where locals and tourists alike can explore an array of fresh produce, artisanal cheeses, and gourmet delights. Here are some of the best markets to experience the local flavors:

1. Marché des Enfants Rouges

- Address: 39 Rue de Bretagne, 75003 Paris, France
- Average Cost: Varies by vendor
- Opening Hours: Tuesday to Saturday, 8:30 AM - 7:30 PM; Sunday, 8:30 AM - 2:00 PM

Marché des Enfants Rouges, established in 1628, is the oldest covered market in Paris. This historic market offers a diverse range of food stalls, from fresh produce to international cuisine. Sample Moroccan tagines, Italian pasta, and Japanese bento boxes as you wander through the bustling aisles. The market's vibrant atmosphere and eclectic offerings make it a perfect spot for a leisurely lunch or a quick snack.

2. Marché Bastille

- Address: Boulevard Richard-Lenoir, 75011 Paris, France
- Opening Hours: Thursday, 7:00 AM - 2:30 PM; Sunday, 7:00 AM - 3:00 PM

Marché Bastille, located along the Boulevard Richard-Lenoir, is one of Paris' largest open-air markets. On market days, the boulevard transforms into a lively scene filled with vendors selling fresh fruits, vegetables, cheeses, meats, and more. Be sure to sample the regional specialties, such as charcuterie from the Auvergne or Normandy cider. The market is also an excellent place to find fresh flowers, handmade crafts, and vintage clothing.

3. Marché d'Aligre

- Address: Place d'Aligre, 75012 Paris, France
- Opening Hours: Tuesday to Saturday, 7:30 AM - 1:30 PM, 4:00 PM - 7:30 PM; Sunday, 7:30 AM - 1:30 PM

Marché d'Aligre is a vibrant neighborhood market located in the 12th arrondissement. The market consists of both an indoor section, Marché Beauvau, and an outdoor section where vendors sell everything from fresh produce to antiques. Sample gourmet cheeses, freshly baked bread, and artisanal charcuterie as you explore the market. The lively atmosphere and friendly vendors make Marché d'Aligre a favorite among locals.

CHAPTER EIGHT
DISEMBARKATION AND FAREWELL
8.1 Saying Goodbye to Your Cruise Experience

As your unforgettable journey along the Rhone River draws to a close, it's time to bid farewell to the floating haven that has been your home. The last evening aboard is often filled with mixed emotions—sadness at the end of an adventure and excitement for the memories you've created. The crew will likely host a farewell dinner, offering a final chance to enjoy the gourmet cuisine and excellent service that have characterized your voyage. Expect a festive atmosphere, often with live music, speeches from the captain and crew, and perhaps even a slideshow highlighting the best moments of your trip.

To make the most of your last night, take some time to reflect on your journey. Wander through the ship's decks, taking in the views one last time. If the weather permits, spend a few quiet moments on the sun deck, gazing at the starry sky and the shimmering river below. This is also a good time to exchange contact information with new friends you've made onboard.

When packing, make sure to double-check your cabin for any personal items you might have overlooked. The ship's staff will typically provide luggage tags and instructions for placing your bags outside your cabin door the night before disembarkation. Ensure that any essential items you need for the next morning are kept with you, as your luggage will be collected early.

For those who have indulged in the onboard shopping, remember to securely pack any fragile souvenirs or wine bottles. Many ships offer complimentary wrapping services to ensure your treasures make it home safely. If you've enjoyed the ship's spa services, consider booking a final treatment to help you relax and rejuvenate before the journey home.

8.2 Disembarkation Procedures: What to Expect

Disembarkation is a crucial part of your Rhone River cruise experience. As your adventure comes to a close, understanding what to expect can help ensure a smooth and stress-free transition from the ship to your next destination. This guide will provide a detailed look at the disembarkation procedures, including the steps involved, tips for a seamless process, and how to make the most of your final moments on board.

Morning of Disembarkation

1. Breakfast Service

On the morning of disembarkation, breakfast is typically served earlier than usual to accommodate the various departure times of passengers. This is your last meal on board, so take the opportunity to enjoy it leisurely. The dining room will be bustling with fellow passengers, all preparing for their journeys ahead. It's a good time to reflect on your trip, say goodbye to new friends, and thank the crew for their exceptional service.

2. Packing and Luggage Preparation

The night before disembarkation, you will receive luggage tags and instructions for placing your bags outside your cabin door. Typically, you need to leave your tagged luggage outside your cabin by a specified time, usually around 10 PM. The crew will collect the bags and transport them to the disembarkation area, where they will be organized by cabin number or color-coded tags.

3. Essential Items

Ensure that you keep essential items such as travel documents, medications, and personal belongings in a carry-on bag, as your main luggage will be collected the night before. This bag should include anything you might need for the day until you are reunited with your luggage at the disembarkation point.

Disembarkation Day Procedures

1. Disembarkation Briefing

On the final morning, the cruise director or a member of the crew will provide a disembarkation briefing. This session is crucial for understanding the steps and timings involved. Pay close attention to the instructions regarding where and when to gather, as well as any specific procedures for your cruise line.

2. Settling Your Account

Before disembarking, you must settle any outstanding charges. Most cruise ships allow you to review and settle your account the night before, either at the reception desk or via the in-cabin television system. Ensure that all charges are correct and that your account is settled to avoid any delays on the final morning.

3. Gathering Point

Each cruise line has a designated gathering point for passengers on disembarkation day. This is typically one of the main lounges or the reception area. You will be assigned a specific time to meet there, based on your departure arrangements. The crew will be on hand to answer any last-minute questions and ensure everyone is ready to disembark smoothly.

4. Disembarkation Process

When it's time to leave the ship, you will proceed to the designated disembarkation point. Crew members will guide you through the process, ensuring it is as efficient as possible. Your luggage will be waiting for you in a specified area, organized for easy retrieval. Take a moment to verify that all your belongings are accounted for before proceeding to your onward transportation.

Transportation and Transfers

1. Arranging Transfers

Many cruise lines offer transfer services to airports, train stations, or hotels. These services can be booked in advance and are designed to make your transition from the ship to your next destination as seamless as possible. If you have not arranged transfers through the cruise line, consider using local taxis or ride-sharing services. For those with later flights or train departures, cruise lines often provide optional excursions or day tours to fill the time. These excursions typically include convenient drop-off at the airport or your next hotel, and prices range from $50 to $150.

2. Airport Transfers

If you are flying out on the same day, ensure that your transfer is timed to get you to the airport well in advance of your flight. Most airports recommend arriving at least two hours before domestic flights and three hours before international flights. Transfer services provided by the cruise line often have fixed departure times, so make sure you know the schedule and plan accordingly.

3. Train and Bus Transfers

For those continuing their journey by train or bus, check the departure times and the location of the nearest station. Many cruise destinations along the Rhone River have excellent rail and bus connections, making it easy to reach your next destination. If you need assistance with directions or booking tickets, the ship's concierge or local tourist information offices can be very helpful.

8.3 Reflecting on Your Journey: Memories and Highlights

After disembarking, you'll have some time to reflect on your journey. The Rhone River Cruise is not just about the destinations but also about the experiences and moments shared. As you travel back home or to your next destination, think about the highlights that made your trip special.

Perhaps it was the serene beauty of the river at dawn, the vibrant markets of Lyon, or the historic grandeur of Avignon. Each port of call offered unique insights and experiences, from wine tastings in Tain-l'Hermitage to the Roman ruins in Arles. Consider keeping a travel journal or creating a photo album to preserve these memories. Journaling your thoughts and feelings about each stop can be a wonderful way to relive the journey long after you've returned home.

Sharing your experiences with friends and family is also a great way to keep the memories alive. Prepare a slideshow of your favorite photos, or host a dinner party featuring some of the regional dishes and wines you discovered on your cruise. Not only will this allow you to share your adventures, but it can also inspire others to embark on their own Rhone River journey.

APPENDIX
USEFUL RESOURCES AND CONTACT INFORMATION

A. Cruise Line Websites and Contact Details

When planning your Rhone River cruise adventure, it's essential to have the right information at your fingertips. Here are some key cruise line websites and contact details to help you navigate your options:

1. Viking River Cruises

Website: www.vikingrivercruises.com

2. Avalon Waterways

Website: www.avalonwaterways.com

3. Uniworld Boutique River Cruise Collection

Website: www.uniworld.com

4. CroisiEurope

Website: www.croisieuroperivercruises.com

5. Scenic River Cruises

Website: www.scenicusa.com

These cruise lines offer a range of packages and itineraries to suit various interests and budgets. Be sure to visit their websites or call their toll-free numbers to inquire about current promotions, availability, and booking procedures.

B. Tourist Information Centers in Rhone River Ports of Call

Exploring the Rhone River and its surrounding towns and cities is an enriching experience, and having access to tourist information centers can enhance your journey. Here are some recommended tourist information centers in key ports of call along the Rhone River:

1. Lyon Tourist Office

Address: Place Bellecour, 69002 Lyon, France

Lyon's tourist office is an excellent resource for information on local attractions, events, and dining options. Their knowledgeable staff can provide maps, brochures, and personalized recommendations to make the most of your time in Lyon.

2. Avignon Tourism Office

Address: 41 Cours Jean Jaurès, 84000 Avignon, France

Avignon's tourism office is your gateway to discovering the rich history and cultural heritage of this charming city. They offer guided tours, ticket bookings for attractions, and assistance with accommodation arrangements.

3. Arles Tourist Information Center

Address: 9 Boulevard des Lices, 13200 Arles, France

Immerse yourself in the artistic legacy of Arles with the help of the tourist information center. From Van Gogh's iconic paintings to Roman ruins, they can help you explore the city's highlights and hidden gems.

C. Recommended Reading: Books and Guides on Rhone River Cruising

For a deeper understanding of the Rhone River region and its attractions, consider delving into these recommended books and guides:

1. "The Rhone: A Cultural History" by Martin Garrett

This comprehensive book traces the Rhone River's history from ancient times to the present day, offering insights into its cultural significance and impact on the surrounding landscape.

2. "Rhône-Alpes (Michelin Green Guide)"

Michelin's Green Guide to Rhône-Alpes provides detailed information on attractions, activities, and dining options in the region, making it an invaluable resource for travelers.

3. "Insight Guides: Explore Lyon & the Rhône Valley"

Insight Guides offer an in-depth exploration of Lyon and the Rhone Valley, with practical tips, maps, and stunning photography to inspire your journey.

Made in the USA
Las Vegas, NV
10 December 2024

13821367R00134